# Doughty Deeds of Musical Valour

## *One hundred years of Southend Musical Festival.*

## *1911 - 2011*

***By Julie Lafferty***

First published in 2011 for
Southend Musical Festival
Southend on Sea, Essex.
by
Dr. Julie Lafferty.



The following gave their kind permission for the reproduction of photographs & images in this book: Echo Newspapers inc. Southend Standard, Southend Musical Festival, Stephen Pewsey, Essex County Council, Southend High School for Boys, Southend Girl's Choir and Southend Museums Service.

ISBN: 978-0-956400-0-1



Printed by Edward Dudfield Ltd, Ilford, Essex.

# CONTENTS

## ***Acknowledgement.***

My involvement with Southend Musical Festival came in 2008 when my son started to compete and I volunteered as a steward in 2009. I was then invited to join the Centenary Sub-committee in 2010. At the first meeting I realised that the Festival had an extensive archive, and as social history is a favorite topic of mine I suggested that someone should write a book! The job was mine!

The first thing I realised was that someone else could take the Archive and write an entirely different book, there is so much material to choose from. As a very new member of the Festival team I approached the Archives with a fresh eye, knowing nothing about the history of the Festival. As a relative newcomer to Southend (17 years only) I found out I didn't know much about the history of the town either!

There are of course many hundreds, indeed thousands of people who have been involved with the Festival in some capacity over the past century. I have tried to capture the great, the good, the not so good but very willing and any event that caught my eye during my research. There will be people and events that I have omitted and for that I offer my apologies, but as any volunteer knows there are actually only 24 hours in a day! (Please don't mention that to Annette as there are at least 30 hours in her average day at the Festival!)

I need to thank all those who have contributed to the creation of this book with their memories, editing skills and encouragement. Special thanks go to Sue Greengrass whose eagle eye spotted the typos and the dubious grammar, and whose dedication to arranging the Archives made this project much simpler for me. Also thanks to Annette and Sally for the benefit of their vast experience of the Festival.

Lastly, I must acknowledge the patience and support of my family - and my husband's culinary skills, without which starvation could have visited the household!

I wish everyone a happy and joyful Centenary Festival.

## *FOREWORD*
## *by*
## *Sir Teddy Taylor,*
## *President, Southend Musical Festival.*

Whilst there are plenty of issues to get depressed about these days, the one event which cheers me up immensely is the Southend Musical Festival - which has now existed for 100 years and which seems to get stronger and more triumphant every year. Of course it is easy to make this kind of optimistic remark about all kind of musical or academic events, but in the case of the Musical Festival, the optimism is shared by many involved in the organisation.

The success of the Musical Festival, apart from the skill and ability of the participants stems largely from the huge amount of hard work and generosity provided over the years by the organisers of the Festival. When the Festival was initiated in 1911 with around 200 entrants, there was a hard working Committee of about 20 adults and 39 volunteers. Now that we have around 1500 entries each year the work done by the Committee and volunteers has increased enormously, and we now have an army organising the event!

It is perhaps wrong to single out indiviudals, but I think it would be unfair not to mention that in the years I have been involved in an honorary capacity, I have been well aware of the magnificent work being done by Sally Browne, Shiela Kelleway, Annette Forkin and Harry Worsfold. Nor should we forget people like Julie Lafferty, who has used her skills to produce a fascinating and detailed 100 year history of the Festival.

Much of the Festival's continued success has depended on the many people who have given a great deal of money to cover the substantial costs of the annual event, and who have financed the costs of all prizes and presentations.

Southend has been more than lucky with the generosity of its community. We start from the list of Friends who pay a fee each year to strengthen the finances of the Festival. In exchange they get admission to all the competitions, and this in turn strengthens the audiences during the Festival. They also have the right to attend the Annual General Meeting and participate in any votes. We are also lucky to have a strong army of professional friends who pay for advertisements in the programmes, and there are quite a few non-musical advertisers such as hotels and accountants, as well as the musical organisations, who never let us down. We also have many people and commercial organisations who willingly provide finance for sponsorship and who have given money to the prize fund. It is perhaps typical of the generosity of the Southend community that when we had a near disaster with a major overdraft some years ago it was all sorted out with speedy contributions from friends of the Festival.

We have also been more than fortunate with the quality of the Adjudicators who use their professional skills to select the winners of the contests. We have invariably been very fortunate with the professionalism and kindness of the Adjudicators and there is no doubt that the high standards displayed here have brought pleasure and help to many youngsters who have learned so much from the advice given to them.

The one problem which we had during our early years was getting access to the right kind of public halls for the competitions, happily the creation of additional premises and halls in the late 1920s helped to solve this.

Looking to the future, it seems clear that the continued success and expansion of the Southend Musical Festival depends on a few strong foundations. First, we need to ensure that we continue to attract the generosity of the local comminuty and local business advertisers. Second, we need to have an army of enthusiastic parents and teachers who encourage youngsters to enter the competitions and achieve high standards, and finally we need to find committed volunteers who are willing to take on the tough and demanding work involved in managing the massive administration required.

We have never failed in 100 years and I hope that the Festival will go from strength to strength.

Best Wishes
from

Teddy Taylor.

## *Doughty Deeds of Musical Valour: 1911 - 1914*

1911 was a busy year for Britain. The coronation of King George V and Queen Mary concentrated the minds of many a local council up and down the land, including Southend-on-Sea, where every child in the borough received a Coronation mug and the Coronation carnival was celebrated with 'unity and heartiness' by the public, as reported by the Southend Telegraph.

The suffragette movement was gathering force, not least in the form of hurling bricks through the Home Secretary's window, earning one Ethel Smythe, composer, two months in Holloway Prison! The National Insurance Act was introduced and MPs were awarded an annual salary - expenses were, perhaps wisely, not mentioned.

On the musical scene, Elgar conducted the premiere of his Symphony No 2, 'Any Old Iron' was published and Irving Berlin brought 'Alexander's Ragtime Band' to the attention of the masses. In Southend, Houdini appeared at the Hippodrome Variety Theatre; the Southend Operatic and Dramatic Society (SODS) were performing Miss Hook of Holland, Southend United made it back to first division football - and a competitive musical festival was being planned.

The origins of the competitive musical festival can be traced to the times of the ancient bards, and the Southend Standard was extremely enthusiastic about the project, citing 'the musical competition, properly conducted, is the greatest work of the day'. In 1907 there were over seventy member societies of the Association of Competition Festivals. Indeed most areas across Essex had established annual competitive musical festivals and Southend was clearly lagging behind in this respect. It was time for Southend to flex its musical muscles, the Southend Standard declaring that there was 'every reason for it becoming an annual affair, worthy of taking place with those other public functions which are red letter days in the diary of the town'.

Southend Musical Council set to work, gathering together interested parties and enthusiastic individuals to make the Festival a reality. The original committee comprised local professional musicians with support from local businessmen. Subscribers were rallied; prizes donated and trophies produced; classes and set pieces were discussed, rejected or accepted and the syllabus was decided - all that remained was to attract the competitors.

The first advertisement for the Festival can be found in the Southend Telegraph of 26th August 1911, giving the date as 11th - 18th November and venues of The Technical College and Masonic Hall. There was to be a prize distribution concert on the 25th November. This is accompanied by a rather enthusiastic article entitled 'Southend's Music Festival - What it will do'. This was to be the first public competition of its kind in the town and the syllabus revealed a 'comprehensive plan of operations'. There were two restrictions on entrants - they could not be professional musicians (other than in designated classes) and they had to be resident in the Parliamentary Division of South East Essex for three months prior to October 1911.

***Fig 1: Technical College, 1905***

95. Empire Day celebrations at the Technical College, June 1905.

As this covered the entire south east Essex area it was hoped there would be no shortage of entries. There were to be thirty-eight classes in all, covering singing and choral, pianoforte, strings, elocution, and theory & composition, giving the competitors the opportunity to distinguish themselves in a wide range of fields. The overall aim of the Festival was stated as 'to encourage the study, performance and appreciation of good music and to afford the competitors the opportunity of having their qualifications tested by eminent musicians'. This aim remains true one hundred years later.

***Fig 2:***
***Southend and South-East Essex Musical Festival Syllabus 1911.***

One such eminent musician was Mr. Henry R. Bird. He enjoyed a long and illustrious career as an organist and accompanist with the reputation of being the finest accompanist in existence! He acted as the organist of St. John's Church, Walthamstow from the amazingly young age of eight, eventually studying under Dr. Turle at Westminster. In 1869 he was consulted on the design of the organ in Melbourne Town Hall and was generally renowned as the very best English organist of the time. Mr. Bird accepted the invitation to adjudicate the pianoforte classes.

Dr. William Gray McNaught was also a highly respected musician and musical scholar, his reputation as an adjudicator for choral work and singing was exceptional. He was a government inspector for musical education and editor of the popular Musical Times. He had been involved in competitive musical festivals for many years and was an avid supporter of budding musicians, always willing to give advice and encouragement. He too accepted the invitation and agreed to adjudicate the singing and choral classes.

Mr. Arthur Payne , a renowned violinist, who had been the leader of the Queens Hall Orchestra and was the Musical Director of the Llandudno Pier Concerts was similarly qualified. With such an exceptional standard of adjudication in place, the stage of the musical festival was set with extremely high expectations for its success.

Responsibility for the success - or otherwise - of the Festival lay with the Musical Council, ably chaired by Mr H.W.L. Hobbs, with the role of the Honorary Secretary being undertaken by a Mr. Alfred Tarling. How these gentlemen came to be involved in this project is not known, but suffice it to say they, along with the 19 strong Executive Committee had taken on quite a task - as current members of the Executive Committee can testify.

In October 1911 the Southend Standard reported over 200 entries for the Festival, fulfilling the 'most sanguine expectations'. Sadly there were no entries for the Male Voice Choir class due to the 'dearth of altos and tenors in the district' and to a 'general lack of ability to read, even decently, at sight.' At least this is the reason put forward by AMICUS, author of the regular Music & Other Things column in the Standard newspaper. The Gold Medal classes of pianoforte and cello were also left unfilled with only one entry in each, and thus the 'handsome medal of Mr. T.J. Gilbert' , owner of a local music shop, was to wait for another year to be awarded. The Charles Waller Shield for elementary school choirs of less than fifty pupils was valued at 10 guineas. Mr. Charles Waller was a local jeweller and watchmaker. He was the official agent to the Festival for the supply and engraving of cups, trophies and medals. Over the past century this shield has been embellished with the winner's medals and is an extremely handsome addition to any school trophy cabinet. The shield, along with a second Waller Shield is still awarded to school choirs. This was one of three shields available in 1911, the others being the Musical Council Shield, awarded to children's choirs, and the H.W.L Hobbs Shield awarded to small choral societies of not more than 30 mixed voices.

The "Charles Waller" Silver Challenge Shield.
Challenge Shield given by the Musical Council.


***Fig 3: Award Shields 1911***

There were also words of wisdom from the newspaper, aimed at the competitors reminding them that the 'sole object is that of mutual improvement - not self glorification'. A special warning was issued to the choirs taking part that is worthy of the full quotation:

> ***' there is more envy, hatred and malice in quires and places where they sing than anywhere else....let one and all strive to combat and destroy any such spirit. There can only be one winner but it is possible, nay essential for one to be able to lose with honour.'***

The article requests that everyone approach the competition in the best and finest sporting spirit and that it be conducted in a 'spirit of the greatest possible fraternity and bonhomie'.

The following week the enthusiasm continued citing the Festival as marking an 'epoch of greatest import in the musical history of the county'. A phenomenon that continues is the rush of last minute entries to the Festival. From the outset very few entries were received until the closing date - in 1911 the entries on the last day were described as arriving 'like a snowstorm, reaching over 200 and gladdening the hearts of those responsible for the venture'.

The reporting of the Festival classes is extremely detailed and AMICUS clearly feels it appropriate to report on the adjudicators' comments and performance, as well as that of the competitors. Mr. Bird refers to a boy in the under 11 years piano playing class as a ***'promising boy who must be an anxiety to his teacher because he was obviously tiresome and lazy'***. The other entrants for this class were more fortunate, being described as 'well taught little angels'. Alice and Violet Longman, who won the piano duet class, were described 'justly' as brilliant, but the entrants of the under 14 years piano class had their efforts to play 'Presto' condemned as a 'runaway taxi cab'. The sight playing juniors were 'disappointing', with first prize going to the child that made the fewest mistakes. Scale playing juniors fared much better, being described as 'good, better, still better, excellent and perfect' with Miss Daisy Vickers taking first prize with 100 marks.

There was some consternation expressed with the senior piano class relating to the choice of music. Mr. Bird was not convinced that Debussy Arabesque No 1 in E was altogether healthy for young musicians, describing it as 'sensuous and ultra sentimental'. Miss Daisy Batchelor was the winner of this class - she also won the senior sight reading class and senior piano duet class. AMICUS ends the review of the piano competition with a ringing endorsement for its success:

***'this revelation of what one might perhaps best be described as domestic talent came as a startling and gratifying surprise...very few of us suspected the widespread musical ability this festival brought to appreciative notice...takes ones breath away and leaves a sensation of pleasurable marvelling.'***

The string competitors fared worse than some of the individuals in the piano classes. Reportedly, the standard of excellence was at a low level, no second prize was given in one class as no candidate justified it and overall the classes were 'lamentable'. Elocution classes were reported as having a 'total want of discrimination between recitation and acting'. Oh dear! This was clearly not a competition for the faint-hearted! However, the readers were advised to ***'take the smackings with brave and thankful hearts' and to see that the festival 'shall have served us well if it but puts our feet on a new and better path. In the next festival we may wipe out the reproach that has fallen on us.'***

The rest of the Festival was reported the following week. It was made clear that the large hall at the Technical College was not large enough, as scores of people had to be turned away from the evening sessions.

The choirs were reported as having 'capital training and much polish'. Again, the selection of some of the pieces was criticised, a folk song entitled 'Mowing the Barley' (traditional - arranged by Charles Sharp), posed particular challenges with Dr. McNaught commenting that ***'many valiant attempts were made to import something artistic into it and slam along with it regardless of consequences of any sort.'*** The winner was awarded 10 shillings and 6d, with second place awarded 5 shillings.

AMICUS felt that Dr. McNaught was not consistent in his criticisms and accused him of 'giving sweets with one hand and smacks with the other', confusing the sense of justice and balance amongst the competitors. AMICUS also took issue with Dr. McNaught over the singing of Handelian solos, Dr. McNaught wanted to hear them 'by the book' AMICUS felt that to sing them this way would 'make oneself ridiculous.'

The first Festival was over, prizes were won, praise heaped, constructive, and apparently not so constructive, criticism was delivered along with some rather harsh observations. It was clearly extremely popular, with people being turned away from both the competition and the prize distribution concert as there was not enough room. The future of the competition was settled - an annual event for Southend had been launched.

**1912**

Britain performed well in the 1912 Olympics with a range of gold, silver and bronze medals in many disciplines. April 12th saw the tragic sinking of the Titanic and Scott reached the Antarctic - albeit to find himself pipped at the post. Italy and Turkey were at war and the Austria-Hungary Serbia conflict was warming up. The unrest however was not confined to abroad, Britain suffered an extremely cold, harsh winter and there was a great deal of industrial unrest throughout the country with strikes in the coal and transport industry and also in the docks. There were organised window smashing sessions around London by the Suffragette movement and Southend had a window smashing incident of its own when Miss Grace Smith, lodging in San Remo Parade, was the recipient of a brick thrown by a neighbour driven to distraction by her excessive piano playing. The local magistrate was sympathetic to Miss Smith, fining the unappreciative neighbour!

Elsewhere in Southend the Palace Theatre opened its doors for the first time and what has been cited as the very first airshow was performed along the seafront, when a collection of seaplanes gave exhibition flights to delighted crowds.

Following the success of 1911 the plans for the 1912 Musical Festival were well underway by the summer. The prospectus was published in July and the dates for the Festival were set as the 16th - 23rd November, with the Prize Distribution Concert to be held on the 7th December. Another singing competition was organised at the Hippodrome for August 1912 but it was not a spectacular success with few entries, despite an outstanding prize of a 60 guinea piano on offer. The Standard drew the conclusion that this competition simply did not hold the same gravitas as that of the Musical Festival and therefore could not attract the quality of performer.

The regular Music and Other Things column for the Standard was now written by a Mr. John Christopher - he may or may not have been the AMICUS of years gone by. He is rather disgruntled by the fact that the committee had made the decision to exclude the winners of 1911 from this year's competition finding it 'somewhat illogical and a cold douche on laudable ambition'.

The Festival was reported in detail and included a range of brickbats and bouquets. Sight playing in the senior piano division was described as a 'painful ordeal' by Mr. Bird who had agreed to adjudicate once again. He also used the words 'disappointing, almost heartbreaking' with the competitors 'unable to recognise rhythm or spirit'. Singled out for comment in the piano class was one Mr. Leander D. Potous, who, according to Mr. Christopher, displayed a ***'strange perversity that caused him to diversify from the music, this disqualified rather than being an easy 1st.'***

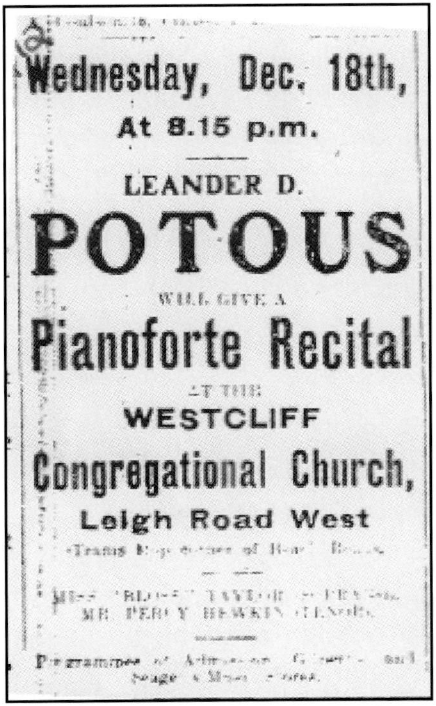


***Fig 4:** **Mr. Potous, advert for his recital concert in the Standard later in the year.***

Mr. Bird also made comment on a very promising young performer - Miss Eveline Booth-Clibborn - who was the granddaughter of William Booth, the founder of the Salvation

Army movement. Her mother was known as the Marechale, a famous evangelist. Eveline was one of ten children in the family, all of whom followed careers in evangelism. Eveline went to the States in her twenties and in a letter home to her mother reports that her music is being well received. She is still listed as a composer of hymns in the Salvation Army songbook. Eveline's sister Frida also took part in the festival.

Once again the Standard took issue with the adjudicators. The elocution classes seemed to receive unusually severe judgement in the opinion of Mr. Christopher. Mr. Stephenson, Adjudicator, found fault in particular with pronounciation of vowels - perhaps he lacked an ear for a true Essex accent! Mr. Payne, who had also returned to adjudicate in the strings classes was also felt to be unfair, only commenting on the actual winners and 'lumping everyone else together for certificates, which must mean very little'. The choice of song in one class - Elizabeth's Prayer from Tannhauser - had Mr. Bantock Pierpoint, Adjudicator and world class baritone, declaring that Miss Vera Williams, a pupil of Mrs. Picken, had 'come through the ordeal gloriously'. However, Mr. Percy Judd was reported not to have put enough effort into his offering with his fine baritone voice.

Overall, the 1912 Festival was once again a great success and a hearty vote of thanks was published to all those concerned.

## 1913

Now an established part of the annual programme of musical events in Southend, the Festival was arranged for 7th - 15th November 1913. A total of 363 entries were received and new classes were introduced in Hymn composition, piano and organ playing. Mr. Bird and Dr. McNaught were once again part of the adjudication team alongside other notably eminent musicians in their respective fields. Mr. Christopher continued to report with relish on the Festival itself and to issue warnings to competitors. Dr. McNaught is reported as 'terse and to the point - if contestants fail to learn something it would be their own fault' ; Mr. Bird is cited as enabling ‘the winners to know why they won and the losers know why they did not’. There was criticism of the syllabus once more with the song for solo tenor noted as ‘not a happy choice’. The stage was set and the arrangements for the Festival were pronounced as providing an ***‘excellent field on which many doughty deeds of musical valour will be performed’.*** One such deed finally came from Mr. Leander Potous, remembered for straying from the written music in 1912. He claimed 1st place with his recital of Chopin’s Fanatasie Impromptu in C# Minor, this time ***‘playing from the music rather than trusting his memory and imagination’***

In the children’s piano sections two sisters stood out as promising, Hilda and Gladys Shrapnell. Gladys in particular was reported as a ‘budding genius’. These young ladies were the granddaughters of Henry Shrapnell, the man who invented the Shrapnell Shot weaponry used to such devastating effect in World War 1. The Shrapnell family have continued to contribute to the arts in subsequent generations, John Shrapnell is a highly respected actor, as is his son Max.

The duet playing class was reported as ‘delightful and instructive’ with Alice Longman and Dorothy Blackwell giving a perfect performance and gaining full marks, whilst the organ class had standing room only. The vocal classes were also well received, although Mr. Christopher proclaims the instrumental talent of the town as far more conspicuous than the vocal, with instrumentalists being created whilst ‘vocalists are born’. Master Lionel T. Waller was assured of a musical future, whilst Miss Beryl E Morrow was described as a ‘dainty little girl whose song was very clearly and sweetly given’. The Charles Waller Shield was won by Bournemouth Park School Girls’ Choir.

The Festival was a huge success - apart from the lack of a suitably large enough hall. Once again members of the public were turned away from the venues due to lack of space.

## 1914

The start of 1914 did not provide foresight into the events that would unfold as the year moved on. The Pier suffered one of its many fires, Southend acquired county Borough status and formed its own police force - the 'Snowdrops' - named for their white helmets - one hopes this was not a direct response to the success of the football team at this time! Troops from the Shoebury Garrison were given permission to drill in the numerous parks of the town - as long as they did not drill on the cricket pitches!

The 28th June 1914 saw the event that was to spark the next four years of tragedy and World War. Archduke Ferdinand and his wife were assassinated at Sarajevo. As the world moved toward war, Britain came to the aid of 'little Belgium', and Southend, like all other towns and cities in Great Britain, saw its young men take the King's Shilling, many in the rush to get to the war that was to be 'over by Christmas'. Prisoner of war ships were moored in the estuary and the Royal Hotel became a naval hospital, housing wounded soldiers and Belgian refugees.

A visitor to those soldiers was a young lady named Marjorie Bose, she would play violin to entertain them. The Festival still has a trophy bearing her name and it is presented to the best performer of the violin / viola class 11 - 13 years.

Plans had been made for the Festival to take place in November 1914, the Annual Meeting of the Executive Committee declaring in March of that year:

> ***'there can be nothing but gratification at the way in which the affair has taken its place as the chief musical event in the life of the Borough'***

The Executive Committee decided to add to its numbers and invited a further twelve musicians to join its ranks. The 7th - 14th November was settled on as the date for the 1914 Festival and two new classes were added: Song Accompanying and Sight Singing.

The minute books from the archives of the Festival are exquisite with copper plate handwriting and precise, formal reporting. However, by April 1914 a formal request was made for the purchase of a typewriting machine. This was approved and a second hand machine was purchased for £5.5.0. Things continued to move apace in preparation for the Festival, the printers of the syllabus were chosen, adjudicators agreed and a solution to the overcrowded prize concert was found by splitting the concert into two parts, Juniors and Seniors. Juniors were to be allowed free admission to their concert, Seniors were however expected to pay for the privilege at half the price of normal admission! Mr. Gilberts' Gold Medal class was still not to be used, although a letter was sent to him thanking him for his very kind offer. Poor Mr. Gilbert had been offering to sponsor a Gold Medal class for pianoforte since 1911, all to no avail it seems, despite being described as 'handsome' in the syllabus and the press!

***Fig 5:***
***Front cover of 1914 Syllabus: 'not used owing to world war 1914 - 1919'***

It was not until September 1914 that it was suggested the Festival be postponed due to the 'unsettled state of the country'. It was felt that early 1915 would be an appropriate time to hold the Festival - after all the war was to be over by Christmas! By November 1914 it was decided that the date should be deferred until November 1915, as otherwise there would be two festivals in one year. Plans were then made to hold the Festival in November 1915.

***Fig 6:* Advertisement in the Southend Standard advising the postponement of the festival.**

In June 1915 the executive committee met once more, and at this point it was clear that the war would continue and that the Festival had to be abandoned for the present. No further meetings were held until July 1919. The first three years of the Festival revealed a wealth of talent, and if not talent, then at least bravery amongst the population of South East Essex and Southend! It had grown into an important and popular event in the annual calendar of the town. From 1914 - 1918 the doughty deeds of valour were to be performed on other fields.

## *In Memoriam*

### *Sergeant Charles James SEARS*
### *7th Battalion London Regiment*
### *(The Shiny Seventh)*

Charles Sears took part in the Festival in 1913 at the age of 19 years. He was known locally for his fine baritone voice and competed in the Quartet of Male Voices class singing 'In absence' by Dudley Buck.

Charles enlisted in the army on the 7th September 1914
and was sent to France in August 1915.
He took part in many battles, notably the Battles of Loos,
Vimy Ridge and High Wood.

He was killed in action on the Somme,
7th October 1916, aged 23 years.

He is commemorated on the Southend Roll of Honour, Priory Park; the County Borough Memorial at the cliffs and on the Southend High School for Boys Roll of Honour.

*Fig 7:*

**Photograph reproduced with kind permission of Southend High School for Boys. First published in 'They rest from their labours'. 2008**

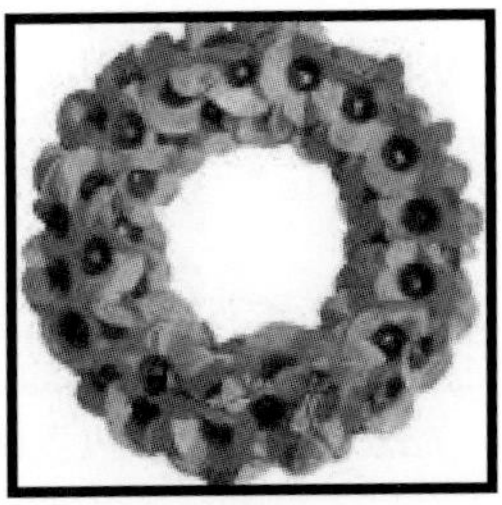

## Southend Music Council
## Executive Committee Members
## 1911 - 1915

H.W.L. Hobbs Chairman (Died 1915)
Alfred Tarling Honorary Secretary 1911 - 1912
Horace Bayliss Honorary Secretary 1913
P.H. Kessell Honorary Treasurer
J.H. Bovenizer Auditor
William J. Barton AGSM
Frank Bonner ATCL
Dawson Freer
C. Turner-Greasley
John R. Griffiths Mus. Bac
Charles T. Loveday
Phillip La Riviere
William Miles
Val Mason LRAM (Died 1914)
Richard Temple
William Whiteman
C. Foster
W. Rudligg
H.J. Teakle
G. Uttley
Mr. Russe
U. Rogers
Irene Foster GSM
Mdm Gertrude Gardner
Marian Gregory
Edith Hammond
Gertie Harrington
E. Duniam-Jones
Ms Ling LRAM ARCM
Jessie McClaren
Ms E. Petit
Mabel Plater LRAM
Constance Parr
Rose Brown
Ms R.M. Harrison
Nora Shears
Daisy R. Walenn
Ms. Jones
Ms. Relgbach

## Twenty Years of Peace:
## 'Haven't you got a hall in Southend?'
## 1920 - 1939.

The siren from the top of the gasworks in Eastern Esplanade marked the end of World War I in Southend. The town had suffered substantial damage in Zeppelin raids throughout the war and many civilians had been killed or injured, but at last the war was over and the peace celebrations could begin.

The 1920s was a contradictory decade in many ways, after the hardships and tragedies of the war people were eager to make the most of their leisure time and be entertained. There were however difficulties to be faced with men returning from war unemployed and mass demonstrations took place across the country in support of their plight. There was a general strike in 1926, and of course, the stock market crash of 1929 left the country reeling once more.

Still, it has to be acknowledged that the 1920s saw the explosion of mass media and entertainment industries and there was an undoubted sense of freedom and frivolity. The cinema developed with sound and colour, Ragtime gave way to Jazz and George and Ira Gershwin wrote arguably some of the most memorable melodies ever heard - even today. The dances were flamboyant with the Charleston, Black Bottom and Shimmy all proving popular in the increasing number of night clubs and dance halls throughout the country - including our very own Kursaal. The fashion reflected the exuberance of peace with young ladies 'flapping' in knee length, shimmering fringes and brimming with the 'Great Gatsby' sophistication and confidence of the day. The rise of the Charabanc and the expansion in transportation and road building all helped to make Southend a buzzing and vibrant seaside town - alongside donkey rides and the Jolly Boys!

*Fig 8:*
*The Jolly Boys*
*1922*

***Fig 9: Southend on Sea Postcard 1920s***

*Fig 10: Thorpe Bay Beach c.1920s*

*Fig 11: Donkey Riding c.1930*

The Southend Musical Council regrouped in 1919 to revive the Festival. Mr Hobbs had sadly died in 1915 and a new Chairman and Secretary were appointed. Alderman Joseph Francis JP OBE took the Chair, and Horace Bayliss took on the extremely busy task of Secretary.

***Fig 12:***
***Horace Bayliss pictured in the Southend Standard, 1921***

The usual business of an Annual General Meeting was conducted at the next meeting in September - the minutes are again written in copperplate - with no reference to the typewriting machine purchased in 1914. However, the 'cash in hand' was reported as £25 16s 6d, new members were proposed and an increase in both the annual subscription and entrance fee was agreed. With these mundane issues settled the Festival was next on the agenda. At first a date of March 1920 was suggested but it became clear that this was too soon and November 1920 was agreed. The 1914 syllabus was to be used and every effort was to be made to 'make the Festival a real peace success'.

In anticipation of the amount of work involved in the organisation of the Festival new council members were agreed and more were invited to join. Mr. Walter Beecroft, although keen to join, was not accepted as a member as he was not a musician nor was he a music teacher, he was invited to become a patron instead and he sponsored a class for a 1 guinea prize. He was later to take part in the Festival as a baritone, singing 'Life & Death' by Coleridge-Taylor.

In consideration of the Festival finances an application was made for music tax exemption and this was granted in September 1920. There was also some relaxation of the rules for music teachers who wished to compete - as long as they were under 20 years of age and taught less than 6 pupils it was felt that they could enter the competition in certain classes. A definition of the professional musician can be found in the minutes of 1922 as someone who used music 'as a means of livelihood'. Although the committee could request a declaration of income from those who were suspected of earning a living from music but not classed as professional.

In 1914 it had been confirmed that Mr. Henry Bird would once again adjudicate the piano classes and it was hoped that he would do so again but, sadly he had died in 1919. This was reported in the Southend Standard in June 1920 alongside the announcement that the Festival was to be revived. Old habits clearly die hard for 'John Christopher' who once again takes issue with the size of the hall ' a pity there is not a large concert hall in Southend', and also with the syllabus: 'preference is given to the English composers', was this wise?, 'surely our attitude should be international?' Another voice of criticism was raised in the form of a letter to the editor, this missive not only dismissed the syllabus but also attacked the 'paltry prizes' and the entrance fees for competitors. This was followed by the accusation that the Festival was a 'quack money-making concern organised to extract entrance fees from deluded and conceited amateurs!' No beating about the bush from this concerned member of the public. Mr. Bayliss answered the criticism the next week with charm and diplomacy letting the facts speak for themselves. Firstly, no good purpose would be served by belittling the efforts of the committee; the syllabus was proving to be interesting and attractive to competitors and entrance fees did not contribute towards the prizes - these were given freely by the generous sponsors of the

Festival; entrance fees had to be charged to cover the extensive organisational costs of the festival, halls had to be hired, adjudicators needed to be paid, syllabus - even boring ones - had to be printed as did programmes. That cleared that up then!

As it subsequently transpired that there were 436 entries for the Festival, Mr. Bayliss must have been very pleased that his rebuttal of such an insult was absolutely correct! The number of entries meant that two more adjudicators had to be found - Edith Hands took on the singing section, a daunting task as in one class there were 31 entries of girls under 18 years singing Frances Dorel's 'The Garden of your Heart'. Written in 1914 this song was very popular throughout the war. Miss Hands is reported as giving the competitors 'splendid advice' and the singing classes overall were reported in a very positive light. Miss Ivy Wright was cited as a 'young lady who is now bound to attract notice on the concert platforms in this town', which she did indeed go on to do. This was her first competition and she won her class with ease.

Miss Wright continued to compete in the Festival as a mezzo-soprano over the next thirty years, she also took a keen interest in its organisation.

MISS IVY M. WRIGHT,
who won the gold medal in Southend and South East Essex musical festival this week.

***Fig 13:***
***Miss Ivy Wright pictured in The Southend Times, 1923***

On her death in 1951 her husband, Mr. John Robertson, donated a fine silver bowl to be called 'The Ivy Wright Trophy' for mezzo-soprano solo. Her son, also called Mr. John Robertson, has donated a very generous money prize to be awarded with the trophy. This has been increased for the Centenary Festival.

Another lady singled out for high praise was Miss Ethel Johnson who according to John Christopher 'took her top note in splendid fashion' and was noted as a 'stylish singer'. A lady who drew particular praise was Miss B Priestley, she was not actually a competitor but she sang for the piano sight reading / accompanying class (Class 45) - in fact she sang the same song for all thirteen candidates! It is known that the piece was to be of moderate difficulty but there is no record of what song was played. Tenor, Mr. Charles Alder was described as a 'really fine singer, soulful and strenuous', with baritone Herbert Allum judged as able to make a success as a vocalist. Even the elementary school choirs were worthy of praise this year, putting up a 'very bright and spirited contest'.

However, as we have come to expect John Christopher was not to let the adjudicator of the elocution classes off the hook, condemning her as 'hypercritical' and judging there to be a 'lack of interest and vitality in the Festival - blaming this on the 'inevitable evil of discontinuity caused by war'. Overall, he declared the Festival a success with many competitors giving promise of becoming 'really good musicians', and of course the committee once again met 'all that was demanded of them'.

The Executive Committee regularly met between the end of the festival and the prize distribution concerts. The minutes make some interesting observations including the receipt of several requests for a refund of entrance money. It remains a mystery why these demands were made but in any event they were refused in 1921 and 'not entertained' in 1923!. Miss Muriel Lloyd had won an award at the Festival but had realised that she was actually a music teacher with twenty-six pupils and therefore not eligible to enter - she apologised and returned her award.

*Fig 14: Sheet music for The Garden of your Heart.*

1921 saw the death of another founder member of the festival committee, Mr. Phillip Kessell. He had undertaken the role of auditor of the Festival accounts since 1911 and is recorded in the minutes as 'an earnest worker on the Executive Committee'. New auditors were appointed with Mr. P. Cannon and Mr. S.J. Strutt taking on the responsibility. Also, for the first time, a consulting solicitor is appointed, Mr. J.G. Drysdale. The date of the next Festival was agreed as October 28th - 5th November 1921 and the venues of the Central Hall at the Boys School and Clarence Hall in Southend were chosen. The prize distribution concert was to be held on the 26th November 1921, although lack of a suitable venue caused it to be moved to 17th December. New members of the Executive Committee were approved, including Mr. James Sears, who eventually became Chairman and was the Conductor of the very successful Prittlewell Glee Society. He was the father of Charles James Sears, mentioned in the memorial to the fallen of WW1 in Chapter 1.

The adjudicators from 1920 were all asked to perform their duties once more and several others were invited to share the load of the 59 classes. Teachers were once again barred from competing other than in Class 27 for musical composition, although Leander Potous, a local teacher, appears once more in a new class for Musical Monologue, he accompanied himself and subsequently 'did not do justice' to the piece -'The Portrait' by Owen Meredith.

The Executive Committee were in for a shock at the meeting of February 1921 - Mr. Horace Bayliss tendered his resignation, citing that the volume and pressure of the work involved was simply too high for him to continue. He excused himself from the meeting and discussions ensued on how to retain his services, clearly an assistant was required, but it was also decided that an honorarium payment of £30 was to be paid to him for his work. Using a historic money converter, this sum is worth £985.00 today - current Executive Committee members take note! It was also decided that in future 75% of the profit made from the Festival was to be set aside for secretarial purposes. This also included 2 guineas to be paid to the official accompanist, Edith Hammond, as an honorarium.

The invitation to take the job of assistant secretary responsible for entries was extended to Mr. Ling who had assisted in 1920 - brother of Miss Ling, another founder member of the Festival. They lived at 59 Imperial Avenue and meetings were often held at their home. Mr. Bayliss returned to the meeting, offered his thanks for the payment and agreed to defer his resignation until Mr. Ling had replied to the invitation. This clearly worked very well for Mr. Bayliss continued in his role as Honorary Secretary and then as Honorary Adviser to the Festival for many years.

Mr. Percy Judd appears in the minutes as a member of the Executive Committee in 1921. He attracted some criticism as a competitor from John Christopher in 1912, but clearly this did not dampen his enthusiasm for the Festival; he now became part of the organisation itself, including composing songs for competition classes. Various competitors from earlier years appear as subscribers or members of the Musical Council and some as Executive Committee members, indicating a strong commitment to the Festival from local musicians. Many of the early competitors moved on to become music teachers and finding themselves barred from competing, decided to be involved in other ways.

By the closing date in October 1921 577 entries were received. It was clear that some classes were now too big to be managed by one adjudicator over 2 days. Mr. Fowles had previously coped with hearing and judging 260 candidates in the piano classes in 2 days! However, at least the syllabus was considered praiseworthy by John Christopher this year - the test pieces were reported as 'chosen with much better care and discrimination. This was evidenced by the recital of Haydn's 1st movement in Sonata in E minor, repeated by 32 -'all consistently good' - 14 - 15 year olds. John Christopher declared that 'one could listen to them all without boredom'. The only general criticism came from the adjudicator and his concerns over the excessive use of the pedal to cover faults. He suggested that 'if the pedal could not be used properly, it should be left alone.' Sound advice! Class 30 was noted as having hardly one incompetent performer and Lorna Fuller-Clark was singled out as a 'finished and artistic performer'. The strings classes were also hailed as a great success, the 14 - 18 year olds were all good. Unusually at the end of the class all the competitors took to the stage and played the piece together under the direction of the adjudicator, Mr. James Browne. This was reported as 'very enjoyable' in the Southend Observer. Although, once again the hall was too small and members of the public were turned away.

There was also mention that there had been no prize awarded in the junior cellist classes. This was discussed at the Executive Committee meeting as some children had scored over 80 marks, but the adjudicator had decided that the performances did not merit a prize. It was decided that the Committee should not interfere with the judgment, but that discussions should take place with regard to setting a uniform percentage across all classes where certificates / prizes could be awarded rather than leave it totally to the discretion of the adjudicator.

Back to the Standard and the exercise of damning with faint praise! The soprano classes were a mixed bag in 1921, Class 11 was 'generally as bad as Class 10 was excellent' and the normally high standard of competition 'did not apply here'. Grace Mason gave the best all round performance and showed a steady improvement from last year with a 'splendid reserve of vocal power', whilst Florence Whiffen endeavoured to put some character into her singing! He does allow that 'some vocalists were somewhat hampered by their accompanists. Class 11 notwithstanding, some other vocal classes received very high praise indeed. The evening soprano class was one of the surprises of the Festival - at least to John Christopher, who ***'never suspected there were so many fine, stylish soprano vocalists in the town and there was not an indifferent singer among the 7 candidates'.*** The tenor class was generally disappointing but Alfred B. Clark with his quiet, refined and temperamental style took first prize with immaculately correct vocalisation. The final class of the evening took place at 10pm and was for the church choirs. Three choirs entered but the second piece performed, 'O Lord, My God', was taken a little slowly for the taste of the adjudicator by all three. John Christopher thought that this was 'probably correct, but there is such a thing as taking liberties with music.' It's very true that one can't please all of the people, all of the time!

Special mention is made of the 'House of Sears' - the Sears family were closely involved in local music events and had entered the competition as a vocal quartet, Father (James), a son and two daughters. Alfred N. Sears had performed in the baritone class singing 'Hope, the Hornblower' magnificently. Alfred can be found competing in the Festival over several years.

The Festival over, the Prize Winners Concert was held on 17th December. The prize winners were to be admitted free this year and again the concert was divided into juniors in the afternoon and seniors in the evening, again this failed to solve the problem of overcrowding! The Mayor, John Francis, arrived late and was immediately harangued over the lack of a decent sized hall in the town. As his predecessor was now the Chairman of the Musical Council, responsible for organising the Festival, he had no problem pointing out that as the new Chairman had not been able to achieve this in several years in office he did not know how they could expect him to! Mrs. Hobbs, widow of HWL Hobbs, the original Chairman of the Festival, had been invited to award the prizes and she closed the Festival for 1921 on this piece of advice to the female competitors:

***'keep up your practice, even after marriage, music hath charms to soothe the savage breast (or beast). When a tired or jaded husband returns from a harassing day of business, first feed him well and then play and sing to him'***

The minutes of 1922 show the Executive Committee agreeing to become members of the newly formed British Federation of Musical Competition Festivals for the sum of 2s per 100 competitors per year, with a liability of 1 guinea should the federation close. This affiliation continues.

The early 1920s saw the Festival continue to grow and the calls for a suitable hall to hold it in grew louder in direct proportion. From 1922 the Festival was held at the Victoria Hall in Alexandra Street. Whilst not perfect, it was certainly larger than the Technical College and once a decent platform had been arranged and everyone was happy with the acoustics, the Festival went ahead at this venue for several years. As other classes were introduced - Folk Dancing for one - other venues were added. Clifftown Church hosted the classes for organ and those for the children's choirs. There was a change for the committee in 1923 as Mr. Francis stepped down as Chairman and Mr. J.R. Griffiths took up the role. Two more shields were added to the growing collection of prizes. One was donated by Mr. Waller giving two challenge shields in his name for elementary school choirs, and another donated by the well known town benefactor Mr. R.A. Jones - again this shield was for elementary school choirs.

*Fig 15: Southend Times, March 1923*

"ISN'T IT BOOTIFUL?"
Presentation by Mr. J. R. Griffiths, Mus. Doc., of the shield for choral singing won by the Chalkwell Hall Schools' infants' choir. Mr. R. A. Jones (donor of the shield) and Ald. H. A. Dowsett are also seen in the picture. (Photo, Southend Times.)

It was also decided that should any choir win a shield three years running then there should be a special award of a mounted and framed photograph of the shield to keep.

Mr. Jones MBE died in 1925 but left lasting legacies to the town in the form of Prittlewell Priory, Victory Sports Ground and the Jones Memorial Ground. The musical shield he donated in perpetuity as patron of the Festival is still awarded.

As well as the Festival there were other events taking place in Southend - the pier had one of its numerous disasters when the Violetta, a concrete bottomed ship, collided with it. King George V took part in the first Southend yachting week, and won with Brittania in 1921. He managed to to take part again in 1923, but this time he ran aground!

In the early 1920s it was decided to hold 'open' Gold Medal classes in each discipline - these classes were open to adult musicians, professional or amateur, resident or non resident. These proved to be very popular and enabled one or two old faces who had left the area to return and perform again. The Shrapnell sisters made an appearance in 1922, 1923 and in 1924, another sister also competed. Gladys won the Gold Medal for piano in 1922 and received a standing ovation for her 'beautiful rendition' of Chopin's Ballade in A Minor'. Her performance was 'brimming over with poetic feeling' - in the opinion of John Christopher. Hilda did not win her class in 1923, nor in 1924 but her effort was mentioned as being one of the best performances. Clearly, there was 'evidently abundant talent in that family'. Muriel, whilst listed as a competitor, did not receive any particular praise.

As each year passed and the Festival got bigger in terms of competitors and reputation, there are many anecdotes within the minutes - still hand written - that are worthy of note but perhaps the most interesting are the records of various disputes that arose. The Festival was (and is) a serious business!

In 1923 the headmistress of a local school wrote to the Committee seeking assurance that previous winners of trophies were not to be subjected to unfair bias, and she suggested that the written rules were not being adhered to. Mr. Bayliss was given instruction on how to reply to this allegation - although the detail of that reply is not noted - one might be forgiven for thinking it fairly brusque as the subsequent meeting noted that the headmistress had written again to the Committee - to withdraw her communication and the entry form that went with it!

Another serious matter regarding the rules arose in 1923 when a member of the public wrote to inform the Committee of a matter of cheating! The junior string trio class had been won not by an amateur as the rules dictated, but by a professional musician. An investigation was carried out. Enquiries were made of the offending child's father, this gentleman was hugely affronted, assuring the Committee that his son was indeed an amateur. He demanded that the Committee request that the accuser withdraw the allegation immediately. As the Committee was satisfied that the child's entry to the competition and subsequent success was legitimate, it was decided to be 'beneath the dignity' of the Committee to enter into any further discussion.

The issue of admission fees for the prize winners at their concert was again given some thought and this time it was agreed that as long as they only wanted to sit in the 2nd class seats, then admission would be free. However, any winner who wished to sit in 1st class seats would have to pay the admission fee. Another aspect to cause considerable discussion was the fact that competitors did not receive the adjudicators criticisms in writing. If any competitor wished to see what the adjudicator had written about their performance they were to pay 1s for a copy. This was not to be resolved until 1925 when it was decided to increase the entrance fees for everyone by 1s to include the cost of the adjudicators written comments.

Folk dancing was introduced as a discipline, the Rayleigh Women's Institute did particularly well in the sword dancing class for several years. Of interest the singing, games and country dancing classes were not allowed accompaniment. It is beyond the imagination of the author to fathom how such dances are performed without accompaniment but rules are rules! The dance classes did prove to be very popular, although the winners did not perform at the prize concerts as - you've guessed it - the hall was not large enough! The dance classes were held at Clarence Hall.

Along with his £30 per annum honorarium Mr. Bayliss was also the proud recipient of a telephone in his home to enable him to continue organising the Festival with 'ease'. This installation was paid for by the Festival. Realisation was beginning to dawn that whilst organising a festival was expensive, taking part in one was not particularly cheap either. Arrangements were made for concessionary rail tickets for those competitors who needed to travel - one gold medal competitor travelled from Leeds to take part. A special voucher was issued and this entitled the bearer to travel as a return fare for the cost of a single fare. It was also decided that any competitor who had to pay for the transposition of music from a certain key, if it was not available in their chosen key, could also be reimbursed that cost. Mr. Bayliss was working very hard to attract as many competitors as possible, especially those for the Gold Medal classes from outside the area. Adverts for the Festival were placed in national journals such as The Musical Times and reminders of the closing date and where to obtain a syllabus were printed regularly in the local newspapers. The syllabus in 1922 contained a foreword with a message to the prospective competitors:

***'If one is not bold enough to run the risk of losing by effort, one can never hope to gain'***

The classes were getting larger with 45 entries for the mezzo-soprano class in 1924 and 781 entries to the Festival overall, this equated to some 71 classes and around 1500 people taking part. In 1925 the entries rose to a record of 880 and the piano adjudicator, Mr. Thomas Dunhill, found himself listening to 444 competitors over 3 1/3 days. The Victoria Hall was again criticised as not being a suitable venue, but with no town hall available it was the best there was.

1925 saw the first success in the Festival by another noted local musician - Miss Freda Parry. The Freda Parry Presentation Bowl is a much contested prize and her name is remembered with affection by her pupils and the local musical community in Southend. On her death in 1971 the Rose Bowl won by her choir at the Festival of Britain national music competition in 1951 was donated to the Festival, and is awarded for the most outstanding all round choral performance. The original Rose Bowl is now on display at the Mayor's official residence, Porters, and a presentation bowl is awarded. Freda Parry also left another lasting legacy to the musical community in Essex in the form of the Freda Parry Scholarship. This scholarship is awarded, via competition, to the most promising young classical singer in Essex. It is fiercely contested, a prize of £1000 plus the prestige of winning the scholarship, is highly sought after.

There have been some interesting dignitaries who were in attendance at the Prize Distribution Concerts, invited to present the prizes to the successful candidates. Sir Landon Ronald presented the prizes at the junior concert in 1922. He had words of warning for the parents of the young winners, advising them not to be too elated by the success of their little darlings, as 'genius was a very rare thing'. He also warned against assuming that a career in music was easily available if all else failed, citing a conversation with a plumber:

> ***Plumber to Music teacher:***
> ***'I want my son to be a musician'***
> ***Music teacher: ' Does he have any musical ability?'***
> ***Plumber: 'No, but there's nothing doing just now in plumbing!'***

John Christopher provided his usual commentary with quotes from various adjudicators and his own interpretations. Mr. Thomas Dunhill, adjudicator of the piano section in 1923 described the metronome as 'a horrid machine but useful in extreme circumstances'; and the adjudicator of the string section stated that the violin was indeed an instrument of 'proverbial torture in evil hands!'

Mr. Leonard Steele won the gentleman's Gold Medal

Class in 1923 and was rather disgruntled that John Christopher had not mentioned his performance and success in his commentary, writing to the newspaper to point out this glaring omission. The following week John Christopher happily corrected this oversight:

***'Gets climax in on 'On away! Awake beloved!' with a burst calculated to waken the dead.'*** Perhaps Mr. Steele should have been more careful what he wished for.....

In 1924 the downtrodden accompanists finally received some long overdue recognition. Mr. Dunhill declared that no more should the art of accompaniment be thought of as simply 'filling in' - the old adage of 'I can't play, but I can accompany' was clearly not true.

Special mention was made of a young girl in the violin class for 10 - 12 year olds in 1924, Diana Kirke, whose playing was reported as entirely delightful. She was in fact almost blind and she triumphed over her great difficulty in an amazing manner, with few members of the audience realising her plight. Mr. Shaw, adjudicator for the choral classes, gave great consideration to the matter of boys singing, suggesting that now women were taking to business and commerce, their menfolk could at last find time to turn their attention to things that really matter - music! It was not ***'an interest apart from everyday life, but a part of the joy of living'.*** He praised the Festival for its accomplishment in bringing boys to 'realise that the energy and vitality which could score a good goal could also be used for the service of music'. He did have stern words in relation to the matter of there not being any decent adult choirs for children to progress to once they had left school:

***'There should be a riot in Southend, the street should run with blood, that in a town like this there are not 20 choral societies to give them (children) a fair opportunity!'***

1924 also saw the demand for a decent town hall reach a fever pitch - the Festival was described as 'handicapped' by the lack of a decent hall. Sir Richard Terry, on handing out the prizes, could not understand why, if Southend could have a fine dance hall such as the Kursaal, why we were not in possession of the hall to which we were entitled. (Loud applause is reported!) The new mayor, Cllr R. Tweedy-Smith, announced in response to the onslaught that 'a step forward had been taken' but refused to be drawn any further. Rumours raged around the town of a site in Victoria Avenue for a new town hall, suggestions were made that some members of the Council finance committee had attempted to 'scotch the idea altogether', and had taken on far too much authority - 'becoming a municipal House of Lords'. Regardless of the rumour and uncertainty, Cllr Tweedy-Smith assured those in attendance that the Festival would be 'held in a town hall with the hearty support of the corporation'.

There was a decline in entries in 1926 leading to speculation about the cause. Could it be the advent of wireless, which according to Mr. Bayliss made for 'listeners rather than performers'; or perhaps it was the proximity to London where a wider range of festivals were available, or maybe the Festival had generally reached its 'turn of the tide' mark. Of course it may well have been a simple case of economics - in 1926 Britain experienced a general strike and times were in fact hard and getting harder. Adjustments needed to be made to attract more competitors. A separate fee was again introduced for the adjudicator mark sheet, so that those who did not wish to pay 1s were not obliged to. The minimum entry number for the Gold Medal Classes was reduced from 12 to 9 and reduced rail fares were again available for those travelling long distances to the Festival. An interesting anecdote appears in the Standard for the 1926 festival with the mention of the 'black cat'. This animal is reported to be well known as a regular Festival spectator and he / she was present to provide another lucky omen. I have found no other trace of this cat but perhaps there was an element of good luck about it as the entries, although lower, were not too bad at 702. The folk dancing classes again proved popular, especially with the little ones, the small girls are reported as entering into every movement with 'great nodding of best hair ribbons'. Entry numbers continued to fluctuate throughout the rest of the 1920s but in general 700 - 750 entries were received each year and the Festival remained stable. In 1927 Horace Bayliss was actually permitted to resign as Honorary Secretary - a role he was to revisit in the future - however, he continued to have an active role on the Committee as Honorary Adviser. Mr. Ling felt unable to carry the whole load and so Mr. Roy Illiffe was accepted as the new Secretary and was appointed Joint Secretary with Mr. Ling. Madame Freda Perry was also accepted as a member of the Executive Committee. In an adjustment to the rules, competitors were now to be allowed to remain in the hall and listen to the other performers and of course the criticisms they received. If they wanted them in writing again there was a charge, but it had been reduced to 6d.

New classes were introduced to attract new choirs and all of the choral and folk dancing classes were now to be 'open'. The Federation made a request for increased financial support and suggested that there be an increase in the entry fee to the competition. This was considered but rejected by the Committee, after all they wanted to attract more competitors not raise fees which would deter many potential entrants.

The previous tradition of holding a meeting between the end of the Festival and the Prize Concert seems to have been dropped and there appear to be no formal executive meetings between October - pre festival - and February / March - post festival. Another change to be noted is that John Christopher's Music & Other Things column in the Standard seems to have disappeared, consequently the tone of the reporting changes to a less acerbic narrative! Although where it was felt merited, criticism was given. Mozart's Lullaby for the under eleven years singing class was 'scarcely suitable .... the average child under eleven has not much use for lullabies, or for bed at all!'

1929 had the Executive Committee looking forward to the time when the Festival had grown to such an extent that it had to be held in the Kursaal. To that end it was decided that the Festival would be open to the whole of Essex and that the name would change to 'The Southend Musical Festival'. This certainly seemed to have a positive effect with entries for 1929 reaching 842. Edith Hammond resigned as the official accompanist after many years of service and was presented with a handsome piano stool. Moving into a new decade the festival was once again growing in popularity in terms of competitors but the audiences were dwindling and the 1929 Festival returned a poor result financially and an overdraft at the bank had to be arranged to meet a few small outstanding accounts. A special finance sub-committee was formed to keep a close eye on the budget. This sub committee came up with several cost cutting measures:

* Return to Victoria Hall - saving of £22
* Change the printer - saving of £20
* Reduce Adjudication fees
* Prize money to be exchanged for cups, trophies and banners only.

A new class was suggested for the 1930 Festival - The Parent Class'. Madame Freda Parry was unimpressed, calling it a 'stunt of no musical value' however, the class went ahead. Mrs. Huxtable won with her piano rendition of 'Autumn', from 'The Seasons, Op136 No 3' by Cyril Jenkins. There were five entries, all mothers, leading the adjudicator to enquire where all the male parents were and congratulating the mothers for having the 'courage to perform in front of their own children.' One would suggest the children were somewhat brave themselves to own up to who their mothers were!

At the beginning of the 1930s Mr Griffiths resigned from the Chairmanship but accepted a position as President of the Musical Festival. James Sears stepped up to the Chair. Once again Horace Bayliss found himself appointed Secretary as Mr. Iliffe stepped down. Business as usual continued, the parents class was discontinued to the relief of Madame Parry and an overdraft of £10 was arranged. It was decided to make a concerted effort to attract more choirs to the competition and Mr. Bayliss wrote to all the local Head Teachers to encourage them to enter their school choirs.

Wider advertising brought results with 14 ladies entering for the Gold Medal class and an exceptionally stimulating Festival was forecast for 1931 with the declaration in the press that 'all roads lead to the Victoria Hall'. Mr. Herbert Fryer FRAM, FRCM Adjudicator for the piano classes certainly had an interesting and somewhat varied time, his only comment for the Bronze Medal class won by Jean Inglis was simply ' That was music!'. The over 18 year class was a little disappointing 'few had insight into the real meaning of the Brahms B flat Minor Intermezzo and Mr. Fryer felt moved to play it himself at the end of class to show the competitors how it should be done. Advice to the scale players consisted of 'put life, colour and purpose into your scales, dead notes never helped anyone.' He suffered a further shock when it came to sight playing. The music chosen was his own composition 'Menuet' and it produced some 'weird and wonderful performances'. He again performed it himself at the end of the class.

Folk dancing was again popular, the little ones were hailed as delightful with 'these small folk literally vibrating with excitement'. For the first time the actual marks received were published in the press, not simply 1st place or certificate performances but the whole class results. A rather bold move and not necessarily one that would make would be competitors rush to enter the competition, some things are not necessarily for the public domain!

There were some changes to the rules and regulations of the Festival throughout the early 1930s, the official accompanist wanted to be able to rehearse with competitors if they wished and this was finally allowed in 1933. Requests were received to advertise in the Festival programme but this was not permitted - an unusual decision in some ways as Festival finances were precarious, but it was felt to be inappropriate other than the advert for Chappells who provided the piano.

Various classes were discussed and tweaked in terms of age limits and selection of pieces. New cups and trophies were donated, the Lester Jones Challenge Cup for church choirs of mixed voices was noted as being of 'a very handsome design'. A rather extraordinary tussle took place between choirmasters in the press. Mr. Thompson, a local choirmaster, did not approve of the selection piece and criticised the length of the anthem, compass of the hymn tune and the overall cost. Mr. Linch, another local choirmaster, answered his criticisms and issued a challenge, pointing out that if Mr. Thompson's choir won the class the prizemoney would cover the costs. Mr. Thompson responded with 'Am I supposed to say thankyou? Choir practice is for church business not competition and the prize money will only buy a larger size hat and pay for a talkie. What would happen if choir members only turned up for the competition practice and not church practice, church business is at risk of being neglected! Members might feel that they 'don't mind joining the choir old fellow, but I'm not going to live at the Church!'. He ended his response with this:

***' All I can promise Mr. Linch is that if I can borrow somebody elses choir for the occasion and he gets away with the prize next November it will be well earned.'***

There is no record of Mr. Thompson's choir entering the competition.

A gramophone was now to be allowed for Country Dancing and the conductor of the Percussion Band class of 8 years or younger could be an older child. Each year saw minor adjustments to the classes and several additional classes. Competitors came from further afield not just Essex, with entrants from Nottingham in one year. The accompanist class continued to stretch the singer to breaking point. In 1932 Miss Marie Jones attracted special sympathy from the adjudicator for what he called her 'stormy adversaries' and 'fighting accompanists', playing for her himself at the end. Ironically, he did not seem to notice that having sung the same song for many pianists she probably did not wish to go through it again! This happened again in 1934 with a different adjudicator, again the song had been composed by him and the desire to play it properly for her was apparently overwhelming!

The performances from the Elementary School Choirs in 1932 again won the hearts of the adjudicator and audience alike. Described as 'delightful' the adjudicator expressed a wish that the older singers should be made to attend to learn an object lesson in 'personality and alertness', these children were 'at a blessed age in music with no temperament and radiant faces'. He told the choirs that 'all that you put into your eyes will come out in your voice' and the older singers 'must be prepared to pay for beauty by the expenditure of emotion'. Although the solo for young boys was criticised as being 'too sentimental for those who begin their career of crime so early'.

Pre festival commentary on the syllabus is detailed and positive, encouraging competitors to enter and the public to attend:

> ***'The music is on the whole, most attractive, after all it is essential to think not only of the victimised candidates when choosing test pieces but also of the hardly less victimised audience listeners' Southend Standard 1933***

Throughout the 1930s the reporting of the Festival tends to review the classes for young children with a great deal of favour. Whether it was a dance class, piano, strings, singing or elocution, the very young children seem to have carried the day; 'shining faces leave no doubt as to their enjoyment'; 'especially praised those with happy faces as well as clever feet'; ' the youngest fiddlers did well and there was nothing of that harrowing discord of wierd sounds that might have been expected'; 'small and dainty as the fairy in the test song'. It appears that Mr. Bayliss's plea to the Head Teachers to enter their choirs may have also influenced the individual entries and the younger competitors seem to have done a great deal to increase the popularity of the Festival still further.

In terms of choirs the Women's Institute and other association choirs really shone throughout the 1930s with classes reaching 13 entries at one point. Dr. Shaw, Adjudicator in 1933, was reported as confessing that he had misgivings about what Institutes were for but music festivals had shown him that 'members did something more than discuss husbands and mend socks'. His overall performance as an Adjudictor was judged as having 'much wisdom well wrapped in humour and not a little satire'. Thank goodness for that it would be awful to think he had been serious! Although he genuinely did not like the 'poor vowelling' of Southenders - or should that be 'Saaarfenders?'

The prize winners concert in 1933 was once again attended by the Mayor and his wife who noted that she herself had competed in the Festival - Daisy Batchelor, now Mrs. H.E. Frith, had competed regularly as a child. This concert included the striking feature of a sword dance to the music of a tom-tom and a mouth organ! The mind may boggle but the concert is reported as a triumphant end to another successful Festival.

1935 was another good year for the festival, not least because of the Royal Empire Day Concert performed in the presence of the King. Mr. Bayliss received a request to put forward ten representatives from the various successful choirs of the Festival to join the national choir for this event. It was a terrific honour and showed the respect in which the Festival had come to be held, not just locally but nationally. To win at Southend was a great achievement.

The piano adjudicator for 1935 was a gentleman named Ambrose Coviello. He proved to be very entertaining in his own right. Discussing the difficulties of hand and eye co-ordination he indulged in a little audience participation. Each person had to grasp their nose with their right hand and their right ear with their left hand, then at his command they were to reverse the position. The extraordinary sight was reported as ***' a melee of***

***grasping hands and twisted fingers which somehow clasped their owners throats, a seemingly ridiculously easy task became hopelessly difficult without practice.'***

1935 was also the year that Peggy Mount entered the elocution classes. Born in Leigh on Sea she was keen on amateur dramatics, starting what was to be her illustious career as an actress at the Wesleyan Chapel Drama Society. Her first attempts at the Festival were not a resounding success, she came last in both her classes! (It is of note that the winners of the class did not become famous actresses). She entered again in 1936 but again failed to impress the adjudicator and was left supporting the other entrants from the bottom of the class. 1937 was not a memorable class either. It was 1938 before she finally shone through and won the Gold Medal Open class with a Shakespearian sonnet and a selection from 'Justice' by John Galsworthy. Peggy Mount went on to become one of Britain's well known and loved actresses, starring on stage, screen and television - younger readers may remember her as Mrs. Bumble in the musical version of Oliver Twist. She was awarded an OBE in 1996.

***Fig 16: Peggy Mount OBE***

FESTIVAL TROPHIES (to date).

Shield—Choral Societies, given by (late) H. W. L. Hobbs, Esq.
Shield—Infants Depts., given by (late) R. A. Jones, Esq., M.B.E.
Shield—Boys Depts., given by Chas. Waller, Esq.
Shield—Girls Depts., given by Chas. Waller, Esq.
Shield—Children's Choirs, given by Musical Council.
Shield—Choral Verse, given by Miss Le Page.
Banner—Country Dance, given by Mr. and Mrs. E. Sharpe, L.R.A.M., A.R.C.M.
Challenge Cup—Country Dance, given by Frederic Gregson, Esq., M.A.
Challenge Cup—Country Dance, given by Friars Infants School, Chelmsford.
Challenge Cup—Mixed Choirs, given by T. Lester Jones, Esq.
Challenge Cup—Pianoforte, given by Mrs. L. White.
Challenge Cup—Choral Verse, given by Miss C. Angel, L.R.A.M. (Eloc.)
Challenge Cup—Vocal, given by Mrs. H. W. L. Hobbs.
Challenge Cup—Percussion Bands, given by Miss H. Thatcher, B.Sc.
Challenge Cup—Dramatic Scene, given by Miss H. Thatcher, B.Sc.

***Fig 17:*** **List of Festival Trophies 1935**

The deaths of Mrs. Hobbs and Mr. Griffiths are reported in the minutes for 1936. The office of President died with Mr. Griffiths. In the same year King George V died and Mr. Bayliss was invited to the funeral.

1936 was also the year of the Festival's Silver Jubilee - it had now been running for 25 years. In 1911 there were 38 classes and 211 entries and it lasted 3 days, by 1935 there were 115 classes and 860 entries over a period of 9 days. Two original members of the committee were invited to distribute the awards that year, Mr. Bonner and Miss Ling. The Victoria Hall - despite being up for sale - was available for the Prize Winners concert. The Festival had gained a reputation for serious work and high attainment and once again was a success. Some 30 choirs took part and Tower House School Choir achieved 100% marks. At the end of the classes all the choirs gave a moving rendition of Brother James' Air, conducted by Mr. Wilson, the adjudicator.

***Fig 18*: Advert for the 1936 Silver Jubilee Musical Festival**

Throughout the latter part of the 1930s various names crop up over and over again, a certain young lady named Pamela Petchy showed much talent over the years, winning prizes in piano and violin. She moved through the classes in turn as she grew older and eventually won the White Cup for two years running. She was pipped at the post for this cup in 1938 by Barbara White but such a great talent was not to go unrecognised - the adjudicator urged the Committee to give her a consolation award for good performance. There was one mark between them. Her scale and sight playing were also of an extremely high standard and she was compensated for the loss of the White Cup with the winning of the Challenge Cup in the Open Beethoven Senior class. She gained 94 marks a clear 10 marks ahead of any other competitor.

The Burridge family also made numerous appearances throughout the late 1930s. Margaret, Joan and Betty appear in both piano and violin classes and they all enjoyed success. Some adjudicators were now hearing the children they had judged ten years ago perform as adults - such was the loyalty to the Festival.

The Festival archives for this period are almost complete, there are syllabus, programmes, Prize Distribution Programmes and most interesting are the records of the official marks. 1936 and 1937 also contain the contemporaneous remarks of Horace Bayliss, not to mention some doodles when there was a lull in the general business of the day! These are the original working copies of his notes on the day, he writes reminders to himself of things that went very well or not so well, who was late, how long the adjudicator waited for them, adjudicator comments and suggestions, mistakes in the programme etc; One mistake in particular came in the Dramatic Scene Class 104, Storrington School had expected to be performing a scene from Black Beard, the little pirates were somewhat suprised to be billed as a scene from Bluebird. Mr. Bayliss also noted that Barbara Shelf 'broke down' - he did not elaborate on whether this related to her car or her performance!

The 1938 Festival was almost postponed as fears grew over the international crisis that year. Germany was demanding the return of the Sudetenland area which had been annexed in the first World War to be part of Czechoslovakia. The potential for another war was looming. On 29th September 1938 a special meeting of the Committee was called and the decision to postpone the Festival was agreed. On 30th September 1938 the Prime Minister, Neville Chamberlain, made his famous announcement:

> ***'My good friends, for the second time in our history, a British Prime Minister has returned from Germany bringing peace with honour. I believe it is peace for our time. Go home and get a nice quiet sleep.***
> **Neville Chamberlain (30 September, 1938)**

The Committee, whilst relieved, did not sleep as advised, but processed the 749 entries and reinstated the Festival in view of the 'more favourable conditions prevailing'. The question of whether the Festival should go ahead in 1939 was raised in March 1939, Germany had invaded the rest of Czechoslovakia and Hitler was making demands for Poland. Despite this the Committee gave a unanimous yes to the Festival going ahead that year. Clearly the Committee were optimistic for the future. Sadly, as history shows, the optimism was misplaced and France and Great Britain declared war on Germany on the 3rd September 1939. The Festival was postponed with great regret, as preparations had gone ahead there were bills to pay and a debt of £28 13 0 was outstanding. This was met with member subscriptions and a request to the 'friends' of the Festival.

It was to be six long years of tragedy and turmoil for the people of Southend and the rest of the world before the next festival would take place. In the meantime Southend was the target of German bombing raids.

Fig 19:
Bomb damage, Southend High School for Boys June 1940.

Fig 20: Southend Home Guard Band 1940

## Revival, Romance & Rock 'n' Roll: 1945 - 1959.

1945 and the war was over. Southend had once again been the target of many bombing raids during the war, with deadly doodlebugs and V2 rockets bringing death and destruction across the town. Southend was a particular target due to its strategic position, the pier, ECKO radio factory (making parts for tanks) and of course the garrison at Shoebury. The fishing boats of Leigh and ferry boats of Southend had played their part in the heroic evacuation of Dunkirk, most notably The Renown, which cost the lives of the four hands on board. Southend evacuated around 62% of the child population throughout the war, mostly to Nottinghamshire and Derbyshire, leaving the schoolrooms depleted. Initially the Council announced that no schools would be open following the major evacuation of children in May 1940, but some did stay open for the remaining children, with trenches and Anderson shelters added to the playgrounds.

Nationally, formal Festivals had ceased throughout the war but once it was over there were soon calls for them to be be revived. The Federation wrote to all organisers of Festivals urging them to take up the cause once more. Mr. Bayliss was again on the case and a meeting of the Musical Council took place to discuss the idea of starting the Festival as soon as possible. James Sears, the pre-war Chairman, had died in 1942 and a new Chairman needed to be selected. This was not done for several months and gentlemen members of the Musical Council took turns in occupying the Chair at each meeting.

An immediate problem identified by the Council was that the lack of children in the town over the preceding years had had an impact on the teaching of music and it had dropped to a low ebb generally. A further question mark was whether another Festival could be financed, there was four shillings and sixpence in the bank and unpaid bills of £10 and 2 shillings! Nevertheless, the decision was a resounding yes to a new Festival and the Executive Committee was formed. New members included previous competitors such as Winifred Nancarrow and Pamela Petchey. The Nancarrow family had been associated with the Festival since 1912 with both Dorothy and Percy competing at that time. Madame Freda Parry and Ivy Wright also continued their association with the Festival.

The first issue to tax the Committee was that of funding and various suggestions were made to ensure the Festival at least broke even. An increase in the entry fee for competitors was seen as inevitable, a reduction in the number of classes would shorten the Festival and reduce the cost of hiring halls and paying adjudicators, and an increase in the subscriptions for members of the Musical Council were all put forward. It was also decided to apply for two grants - one from the Federation and another from Southend Council - neither of which came to fruition! Finally, a guarantee was to be requested from members of the Musical Council should the Festival make a loss.

Over the next few meetings the dates were set, sub-committees were formed to select test pieces and 37 classes were deleted from the syllabus, including the duet for two pianos. Mr. Bayliss was given 30 shillings toward the cost of his telephone bill per quarter and debate over where to hold the festival continued. Just like old times!

In April 1946 the death of Miss Ling - an original member of the Executive Committee - was reported, as was that of Mr. Lester-Jones, Honorary Secretary of the London Music Festival. Later that year Councillor Renshaw accepted the invitation to become Chairman of the Executive Committee. He was eventually to become Mayor of Southend in 1951.

The 1946 revival Festival was a great success both for the competitors - there were 749 entries - and in financial terms; once all bills were paid there was a reasonable balance in hand of £106.00. It would have been a little more but Frederick Moore, the piano class adjudicator, had demanded a further two guineas in fees as the work done warranted further remuneration in his opinion! The 1946 Festival program stated that some 15,300 competitors had taken part in the Festival since its beginning in 1911, confirming its popularity. Hilda Nevard won the ladies Gold Medal, Singing and a new generation of performers were introduced to Southend. Media coverage was not nearly as thorough as in the previous years of the Festival with only a few paragraphs detailing the event and long lists of results. However, the Festival was back and plans continued for the next one.

As each year passed the Committee reviewed the Festival and made adjustments to the rules and regulations as necessary, giving thought to its attractiveness to both competitors and the public. An approach was made by a recording studio in 1947 to come along and record the contests, after much debate and consultation with the Federation it was felt not to be in the best interests of festivals in general and the request was declined.

Of note throughout this period is the success of the St. Bernard's Convent School both in choir and elocution classes; first prizes, cups and trophies all went their way. Some soon to be familiar names also began to appear - Gladys Mu'dd (Mude), an accomplished soprano, competed over many years and won in several classes including the Gold Medal and Challenge Cup. Again, this was a family affair and Gladys's mother, Daisy, donated the Mude Cup, after many years of serving as a volunteer at the Festival. This cup is still awarded. The Willison boys also made their debut in piano, violin and singing. David, John, Peter and Edward became regular performers throughout the 1940s and 50s. A further connection with the Festival came in the form of a Memorial Cup for their mother Kathleen Willison, a member of the Musical Council. The Waller and the Frith families continued their involvement; again both families have donated cups to the Festival. The Wallers and the Willisons are joined by more than the Festival as Pat Waller became engaged to John Willison.

The Prize Winning Concerts continued to cause problems in terms of accommodation and were now to be divided into three separate events, with two junior concerts and one senior performance. A spacious venue was still not in existence and the committee wished to avoid the overcrowding and complaints of the past.

Over the next few years as the 1940s drew to a close several new cups and trophies were donated and the Festival continued to grow. The 1948 Festival received 1113 entries and in 1949 an astonishing 56 choirs entered the competition! One choir was unfortunate in having half their singers - mostly the men - caught in fog on a coach somewhere between Southend and Ockenden, the half of the choir that were at the venue continued their performance regardless!

***Fig 21: Daphne Ventris, winner of the Chopin Cup 1948.***

Of interest from the 1949 Festival is a letter from the adjudicator of the singing and choral classes, Maurice Jacobson. He complimented the school choirs in particular citing a ***'healthy competition in a time of the non-competitive virus that undermines the whole school musical health of the country'.*** The fashion for non competitive activities it appears was not invented recently. Ambrose Marriott, Adjudicator of the elocution classes also felt moved to write to Mr. Bayliss post festival, he stated:

*'I remember with particular pleasure the originality, vitality and courage shown in the choral speech classes.'*

The reporting of the Festival did pick up a little in 1949 with Bert Holliday writing a lengthy article on the proceedings. His son, Jack, had entered the competition as a baritone and on winning his class was singled out for particular praise by the adjudicator. Dad was clearly very proud.

1949 also saw Ralph Vaughan Williams become President of the Federation and HRH Princess Elizabeth become the Patron. Also another stalwart supporter of the Festival, Mr. Chas Waller, passed away in 1949.

1946 - 1949 had been years of revival that put the Southend Musical Festival firmly back on the map. Maurice Jacobson had also described the Festival as 'one of the best in the country' and praised the spirit shown throughout by the competitors. The original aims of the Festival remained and the challenge of competition continued to prove attractive and educational. With more cups and trophies, and increasing numbers of competitors and audiences, the 1950s beckoned.

Renowned in history as the decade when rock and roll took a hold of teenage culture and jived its way into all sorts of trouble the 1950s was vibrant, loud and rebellious and generally prosperous - not unlike the 1920s! There were far-reaching changes happening across the world both socially and politically. In medicine the first organ transplant was carried out, Watson & Crick discovered DNA and the polio vaccine became available - life saving developments. America saw the civil rights movement gather force, Rosa Parks refused to give up her seat on the bus to a white person and the rest is history; Winston Churchill once again became Prime Minister; colour television made its debut; the coronation of Queen Elizabeth II took place and seat belts were introduced - to name but a few. However, the name on everyone's lips - whether in swooning support or spluttering outrage - was that of Elvis Aaron Presley. He burst onto the international stage in the mid 1950s and popular music was never to be quite the same again. Jazz gave way to 'cool jazz' with Miles Davis and Ella Fitzgerald; the blues became rhythm and blues with Little Richard, and the crooners continued to croon. The Amercian influence seeped through via Cliff Richard and Bill Haley, the hit parade was well and truly established. Locally there were some key events throughout the decade, not least the great smog of 1952 that engulfed London and was responsible for the deaths of some 8,000 people in total and of course the floods of 1953 that claimed 58 lives on Canvey Island. The cliffs suffered a landslide, the bandstand (wedding cake) was demolished and of course no decade would be complete without the pier catching fire!

The Musical Festival continued to focus on what is best described as formal, educational music and drama - classical composers and Shakespeare were key, and although folk songs and folk dancing were included, again these were of the traditional old school formats. It was to be many years before the classes of the Festival included the popular culture of the day with classes in modern ballads and jazz. Despite this, entries remained above 1,000 in each year throughout the 1950s and the Festival maintained its popularity.

***Fig 22: Southend Bandstand***

The Festival of 1950 had an added dimension, the winners of certain classes were to be put forward for the

National Competition to take place at the Festival of Britain celebrations in London in 1951. The number of entries for choirs surpassed that of 1949 with 77 choirs, incorporating some 1,700 singers, competing for the opportunity to go forward to the Royal Festival Hall. Madam Freda Parry took first place, not only at the Southend Festival but as mentioned previously, her choir won the rose bowl at the Festival of Britain as well. Other Southend winners also went on to be successful at the 1951 competitions with Elaine Burrough winning the oratorio class, the Nazareth House Junior Choir won 1st prize in the under 12 years category and the Wesley Dramatic Society also achieved first place. The Festival of 1950 and subsequently the National Festival of 1951 were a resounding success for the musical talent of the town.

***Fig 23: Festival of Britain logo, 1951.***

1951 was an important year for the Festival not simply because of the opportunity afforded by the National Festival but it had also reached the milestone of its 40th birthday. Sadly, this was also the year that Ivy Wright died. Bert Holliday was reporting on the Festival and some of the old style reporting was once again apparent. He comments that Horace Bayliss ' never seems to tire, or even rest from one year's end to the other' and referring to the amazing confidence of young performers these days he states:

***'the maiden voice echoed through the memorial hall as if it was the song of an angel. Indeed, one of the old school - a robust soprano of the fat and forty breed of musicians said ' these young competitors have no nerves at all!'***

It seems that the bravery of the youngsters in the 1950s would have been viewed as impudence in previous years and not at all acceptable, but was now seen as characterising a new boldness of spirit and confidence. Bert did feel that the adjudicators were harder to please than in previous years and that they gave low marks in general. He found this particularly galling:

***'Dash it all, I think that if a singer is worth his salt at all in a championship class he should be given at least 90%'***

His son had won the Gold Medal that year with a rendition of Hiawatha's Vision by Coleridge Taylor, but it is one of the few classes that year where the actual marks for the competitors were not recorded on the official program. It might be a reasonable assumption that young John had not achieved 90% despite winning the class!

A class introduced in 1951 that was to grow in popularity was the National Dance class. There were four classes encompassing an age range of 6 - 18 years. The dances came from Poland, France, Hungary, Austria, Norway, Scotland, Italy, Estonia .......in fact it appears to have been a world wide affair. There were also operatic and character dance classes that proved to be very popular. The very young competitors never failed to charm both audience and adjudicator.

***Tarantella***

***Scottish***

***Austrian***

***Fig 24: National Dance Costumes.***

The business of the Festival continued apace with an emergency Committee meeting that year mid-Festival. The emergency Committee met whenever there were urgent matters that could not wait for a full Committee meeting. One such urgent matter was that of a young dancer who had won her class, she requested that she be allowed to take the cup before the official award concert so that she could be awarded it at her own dance school presentation! Due consideration was given to the request which was then given a very firm no! It seems the 'bravery' (also known as impudence) was not confined to the singers!

The ladies' Gold Medal vocal class of 1951 received record entries of 24 and required an entire evening session to hear them all. The large classes of very young children also caused some consternation as to the effect of competing and the impact of adjudication on impressionable young minds. Very careful handling of these young children was required - the minutes comment that this careful handling should also apply to the 'somewhat anxious parents'; there are no specific details about exactly what form this careful handling was to take.

Federation business centred around the idea of setting a national standard of marking, especially in classes where medals and trophies were at stake. There was no uniform standard nationally that would ensure a competitor who scored highly would receive the cup, medal or trophy, this was often left to the adjudicator's discretion. However, it meant that in some festivals trophies were awarded for lower marks than in others. This question was not resolved at this time and it was to be many years before it was!

The 1952 minutes take up the rather odd question of what to do about the members of the audience who liked to knit throughout the sessions. Miss Nancarrow had had enough of the clicking of the needles and complained that it was extremely distracting. The Committee, whilst happy to consider a restriction on the practice of knitting, could not actually come up with a satisfactory solution so the booties, bonnets and blankets etc continued to be produced. Perhaps a unique percussion class could have been established purely for the click clack of the knitting needles!

The minutes of 1952 also remind the Committee that the selection of test pieces was to be treated with the utmost secrecy so that these were not known to competitors prior to the publication of the Festival syllabus. There were no actual complaints recorded about this but clearly it was, and still remains, an important part of the organisation of the Festival to ensure that no one has an unfair advantage by gaining early knowledge of the test pieces.

The passion for choirs also continued into this year with 79 separate choirs taking part. The organisational skill required to accommodate such numbers must have been phenomenal! It is easy to see why there was no venue large enough to cater for the sheer numbers of people competing, the scheduling of the classes had to be undertaken with military precision to ensure that all ran smoothly. Whilst this took an army of volunteers to manage there is no doubt that Horace Bayliss was the Major General who ensured such seemingly effortless magic. In 1952 he finally had the time to devote himself fully to the Festival as he retired from his full time position with the Council Treasury department.

***Fig 25:* *Horace Bayliss, on his retirement, slightly older but no less enthusiastic!***

The prize distribution concert of 1952 was once again a sell out success and the now rather repetitive pleas for a decent concert hall were again voiced. Mayor Longman JP described it as a 'crying shame' and felt that if a decent town hall existed it would be a centre of culture for music and drama for the town. It would accommodate 'four times' as many people, instead of which large numbers were barred from attending such wonderful entertainment by lack of space. He also mentioned that the adjudicators that year had commented on the 'improvement in deportment and platform manners of competitors'. Perhaps he wished to reassure interested parties that should such a marvellous venue ever exist the competitors would know how to behave in it!

1953 was another celebratory year for the country and the Festival. It was the coronation year of Queen Elizabeth II and special classes were held in honour of the occasion with a coronation memento and increased cash prize.

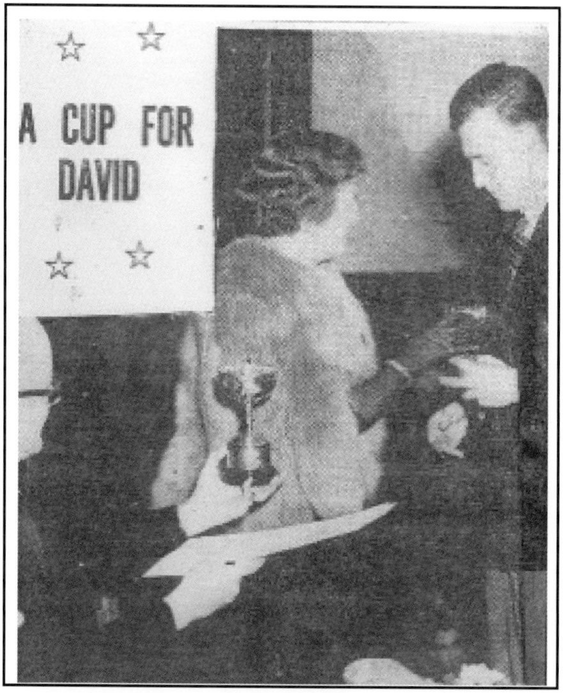


***Fig 26: The Mayoress of Southend presenting David Willison with the Eleanor Button Challenge Cup. 1953***

The standard of competition was reported as being 'as high as it had ever been'. Freda Parry again enjoyed both local and national success in festivals and her choir were referred to as ‘Southend Ambassadors of Song’. The Willison family were also very successful in this year with David winning the Eleanor Button Challenge Cup for his delivery of a Beethoven Piano Sonata. Peter Willison took first prize for the Violoncello class and his brother John won the Neath Violin Bow. David and John also won the chamber music challenge cup as a duet and David achieved the Gayler Challenge Cup for his duet with Aideen Tolkin. As has been noted about previous groups of siblings - this was a somewhat talented family. The high standards were again reflected at the prize distribution concert, as was the overcrowding. The chairman giving the awards that year, Mr. Henry Cloke, Headmaster of Westcliff High School for Boys, commented that it took him ***‘ten minutes to get inside the building because of the crowds and I am the Chairman!’***

In the same year the area committee for the Federation requested an £8 guarantee and £150 donation to the running of the national competition in 1954 and, whilst Southend had supported the National Competitions in the past, it was felt that the cost could not be justified this year. It is clear that from the very start of the Festival in 1911 the governance of the financial aspects of management was rightly very strict and each request for support or expenditure was discussed in detail before decisions were made. This remains true - as Trustees of the charity, the Committee is responsible and indeed accountable for all expenditure and the correct discharge of that duty is vital for the reputation and governance of the Festival.

The emergency Committee meeting of 1953 centred around a complaint about how a small choir had been ‘manufactured’ from a larger one and was therefore not really a genuine small choir, as was meant by the spirit of the class. The rules on this were clarified for the next year and a small choir was required to be just that and not a group of singers selected from a larger choir specifically for the purpose of entering the class.

The 1954 Festival had some controversy in the Drama section. The Wesley Dramatic Society won 1st prize but were disqualified following a complaint that one member of the cast was underage at 16 years old. The runners up were the Westcliff Townswomen's Guild but they refused the prize and chose not to perform at the prizewinners' concert.

The reporting of the 1954 Festival was quite detailed and the elocution classes were clearly impressive ***'at a time when there is much condemnation of slovenly speech it was heartening to hear the adjudicator's opinion of the diction of the children'.*** No sloppy Saafend vowels this time!

The ladies' Gold Medal was won by Dorothy Perry singing Verdi's Ritorno Vincitor. She was awarded 92 marks for a 'brilliant performance with impeccable Italian'.

Whilst not wanting to take anything away from the reporting of the Festival itself, the outstanding news of the Festival in 1954 was the announcement at the Prize Distribution Concert that permission for work to commence on the Shorefield Pavilion had been received from the Ministry of Housing and Local Government. The Pavilion was to be the new home of the Festival. At last Southend could say 'Yes - we have a hall!'.

Several new classes were introduced for the 1955 Festival and some reinstated from previous years. The song accompanying at sight class was brought back with some lucky singer getting to repeat herself 15 times over! This year it was Gladys Mude - a past winner of several classes and cups including the Gold Medal classes. Miss Mude had lived in Southend since the early 1920s, moving to Bedford to train as a teacher but even then she returned to enter the open Gold Medal class during her time away from the town. She was trained as a singer by Madame Freda Parry and also trained in piano. She continued her interest in the Festival and music in the town in general, becoming a successful choirmistress herself, conducting the Nurses' Choir and winning the Stratford Competitive Music Festival choral class three times in the 1960s.

***Fig 27:***
***Miss Gladys Mude, MBE at the 2010 festival with the original Mude Trophy.***

Back to 1955 and the new classes proved to be successful, including the conducting class where a small choir was chosen by Madame Parry and rehearsed in the selected test piece. The choir would then be handed over to the would-be conductor for the performance at the competition. A theory class was also introduced and well-received that year.

As mentioned before, the organisation of these Festivals was always challenging, and as well as the core Executive Committee and their given responsibilities, there were many other people working behind the scenes and in front of house to ensure its success. The stewards were, and still are, all volunteers, as are all the Committee members. Competitors needed to be shown where to go and told when they were to perform, audiences needed to be seated and of course ticket money had to be collected. Each year a small army was (and is still) required. In 1955 it was decided that a stewards sub-committee was needed to organise the timetable of the volunteers.

In the later years of the 1950s the programme starts to include advertising. Most of the adverts were from firms that could supply materials for performers in one form or another. Wades could supply everything from musical instruments to theatrical wigs and costumes and Birn's - a gentlemen's outfitter - also provided badges from school to regimental blazers. Joyce and Bobby Birn were connected to all of the musical events in the town and Bobby served as Chairman of the Musical Festival for several years. Grindleys could supply you with the Festival programme, syllabus and of course books; Currys and Cooper Brothers were also advertisers. Of interest was the advert for the Corporation Bond. This was now running at 5.4%, invested for 7 years with a guaranteed no capital loss; if only they were available to the investors and savers of today!

In 1956 consideration was given to extending the geographical scope of the Festival to all classes, but it was decided that it should remain unchanged. To encourage competitors from further afield the selection committees could change the status of some classes to 'open'. Mayor Renshaw now stepped down from the Chairmanship and Wilfrid A. Waller took up the role. Despite the success of the new theory and conducting classes the previous year there was only one entry in each class for the 1956 Festival, so they were deleted from the programme. Song accompanying at sight had only two entries and was deemed to be unpopular. The elocution classes were a huge success, even the Gold Medal class proved popular and the medal was actually awarded. It was reported as an ideal subject for teaching in schools, improving children's diction and voice production.

The singing Adjudicator took a novel approach to judging the Men's Gold Medal class by asking the audience to indicate their choice of winner by a show of hands! Thankfully the audience proved to be 'attentive and knowledgeable' giving the same answer as the judge and awarding the medal to David Green of Thorpe Bay for his performance of The Dream from Manon by Massenet.

Margaret Murray was also a highly successful competitor in 1956. She had entered the Festival over a period of several years but in 1956 she scooped four of the senior piano cups. There was also the rather amazing winners of the Ballet duet class - Nicholas Benton and Michael Coleman. The dancing classes were always predominantly female, so the boys really put on a brave and evidently prizewinning performance.

In 1957 the Elocution classes were rebranded as the more modern 'Speech and Drama' classes. Recorder classes and a new Accordion class were also to be introduced. It was of some concern that the income was not meeting the costs of the Festival. Programmes were selling at a loss and it was decided to increase the cost of the programme, syllabus and the entrance fees for some of the classes. Another source of belt tightening came from charging competitors some of the cost of engraving the cups, trophies and shields. The Committee would donate five shillings to each item that required engraving but the rest had to be paid for by the winning competitor. It is also noted in the minutes that Mrs. Chas Waller had celebrated her 90th birthday.

A very unusual and novel form of trophy received its first outing at the 1957 Festival, this was for the Quartet classes. The Pett trophy was actually four small cups - one for each competitor. Entries were a little lower at 1,173 this year but still above 1,000. A wave of Asian flu had caused a considerable amount of illness throughout the town. Despite this the new accordion class proved to be very popular with some 31 entries and the Bach Junior Cup was of such a high standard that the Adjudicator announced that all four performers would win prizes in any festival.

With the large numbers of competitors and many classes to cater for, the Prize Distribution Concert was becoming more difficult to co-ordinate and plan and it was felt that the time between the end of the Festival and the Concert should be at least one month. The Concert now consisted of four separate events - two juniors, an intermediate and another one for the senior competitors. The problem with this decision was that the prizewinners wanted their prizes more quickly, had moved on to other work and were reluctant to come back and produce their prizewinning performance a month later. However, if they did not turn up they did not get their prize.

No stranger to prizes, Gladys Mude continued to win cups and trophies as the decade drew to a close, both as a soloist and in the duet classes, her speciality being the British Folk Song. The Willison family continued to perform with Peter taking the Nancarrow Challenge cup with 95 marks in 1957 and brother Edward winning his strings class.

By 1959 70% of competitors were gaining 80+ marks. The Festival had established itself once again as one of the finest in the country with high standards and exceptional performances.

***Fig 28:***
***'How lucky you are to have so many fine singers'***
***Dr. Herbert Wiseman congratulates Edith Day, Conductor of the Southend Central Townswomens Guild Choir on winning the Madame Radcliffe Lewis Challenge Cup.***

***Fig 29:***
***Novice Class with Mr. David Martin, Adjudicator (1959)***

*Fig 30: Southend (Central) Townswomen's Guild Choir (1959)*

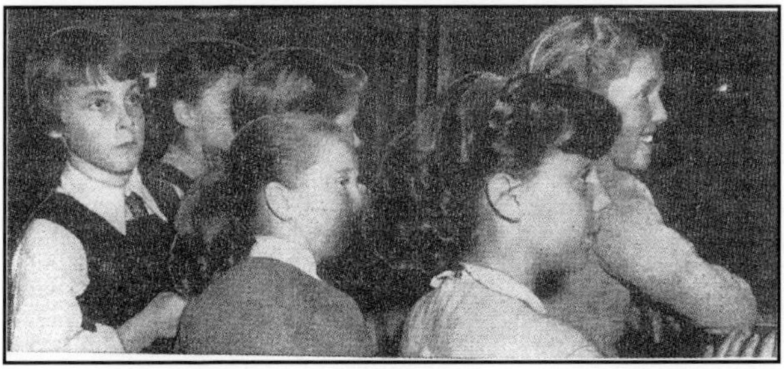

*Fig 31: Waiting for trouble...... solo mime competitors (1958)*

*Fig 32: St. Bernard's Convent High School. Winners: Choral Speaking (1958)*

*Fig 33: Last minute cramming 1948*

***Postscript:***

***Miss Gladys Mude MBE sadly passed away in June 2011.***

## Singing and swinging!
## 1960 - 1969

The 1960s were every bit as lively as the 1950s in Southend. The Cliffs Pavilion opened and attracted some of the now legendary names of the day - the Rolling Stones and Roy Orbison. The Beatles appeared at the Odeon. James Bond aka Sean Connery could be seen driving the 007 Aston Martin around the airport en route to Switzerland and Queen Elizabeth the Queen Mother opened the Civic Centre in Victoria Avenue. Fings were definitely not wot they used to be and parking meters were indeed placed outside our doors to greet us!

The Musical Festival continued its work and Horace once again tried to resign his post as Secretary and once again agreed to stay on for one more year on condition that suitable and reliable help could be found. David Willison now made his appearance on the Executive Committee and Winifred Nancarrow stepped down.

The business in hand at the start of the decade remained the standardisation of marks and this matter was still under discussion at the Federation. The usual review of classes took place with both the song accompanying and public speaking classes removed from the syllabus.

The Festival got off to a great start in 1960 with 1,185 entries and Maurice Jacobson, Adjudicator, Choral and Singing, and some of the piano classes pronounced it as one of ***'the most heartwarming and satisfying festivals I have witnessed.... children gave an enchanting performance and I feel that many of them were born to sing'.***

The Federation had issued new marking sheets, going some way to standardise the marking system. This however did not help in the award of the Willison Cup - three competitors received a mark of 86 in their respective classes and each could have been awarded the cup. It was decided that none would have it as it had to be won outright.

The programme for 1960 was particularly well annotated by Horace giving great detail and anecdotes for the event. The choice of ‘La Gitana’ (Tango) by G S Mathus for accordion was described as ‘totally unsuitable’ by the Adjudicator, and ‘Shopping’ the test piece for the 9yr old pianists found some of them shopping too quickly and others too slowly!

Below: Talking to four young competitors at the Festival on Friday is Mr. Maurice Jacobson, B.Mus., A.R.C.M., Hon.F.T.S.C., who judged the pianoforte section.

***Fig 34:***

***Maurice Jacobson.***

Elfin Dance by Jensen had been chosen for the 14 - 15 year old pianists and the Adjudicator commented that he ‘had never heard it done well at a Festival’, nevertheless Elizabeth Anne Smith scored 89 marks so one hopes she played it well enough! The singing classes attracted many of the now well known sopranos in the district, Margaret Cozens, Dorothy Havis and of course Gladys Mude - who was successful winning the Hobbs Challenge Cup, the Gilberts Challenge Cup and the unaccompanied song class. Lynnette Elliott and Susanne Heath were informed that at 14 years of age they had ***‘great promise for the future, as showing professional ability - if you work!’.*** Alan Girling played violin with ‘great beauty, every promise of making a fine violinist’ and overall the competitions reached an ‘astonishingly high standard’ this year.

Poor Brenda Street deserved a prize for simply turning

up; she had fractured her jaw five weeks before the festival with the wires removed just 3 days before, and the splints were still in place. She entered classes in singing, piano and flute! Had she remained at home she would have received a message of sympathy from the adjudicators as did two other girls who had sustained accidents before the Festival and could not compete. The minutes note this as a 'nice gesture.' Brenda continued into a professional music career as an examiner for the Royal Academy of Music.

A local girl who started to compete at this time was Vivienne Clulow, she took no less than five prizes in various classes in 1960. She attracted high praise from the adjudicator in Speech and Drama winning the W. Camm Bacon Memorial Cup in the under 8 years old class: ' very brave - no prompting!'.

***Fig 35: Vivienne Clulow, Competing at festival.***

Vivienne, now Mrs. Cunningham, continues to be very involved in the local community in Southend. She was, for several years, the Convenor of the Speech & Drama section and continues to be a well respected local Speech & Drama teacher, achieving many successes with individual pupils and group-work at the Festival.

Throughout the year no suitable assistant had been found for Horace and in 1961 he stuck to his guns and resigned. Mrs. Sita Lumsden finally accepted the challenge and Horace, in recognition of his 'long and faithful service over 48 years', was rewarded with the 'new' post of Honorary Adviser - a role he also took up on the last occasion he resigned!

1961 was the Golden Jubilee year for the Festival. The syllabus was to be a fluorescent blue with gold lettering, there was to be a special certificate and increased prize money in some classes. A Social Committee was formed to organise a reception with buffet and a short musical programme to be given by eminent past competitors. The Festival Jubilee Evening was to consist of a display of the Festival records, a supper and speeches. (Not dissimilar to the current plans for the celebration of the centenary year!) Mrs. Waller made and donated the cake and the entertainment was provided by the Freda Parry Choir and the Willison Trio. Horace responded to the toast and 'reminisced to the delight of all'. The newspaper reported on the Festival as usual adding that in this, the Golden Jubilee year, ***'only one dream remains unfulfilled - their hope for a large hall in central Southend where competitors and audience could be accommodated in comfort.'***

Entries for the Festival that year topped 1,300, with 151 classes, and speech and drama classes were especially popular. Again the adjudicators gave high praise. This time it was Muriel Staveacre who noted that ***'academies are lucky to get people with years of training behind them such as go through this festival.'***

For some reason no time limit was given for the Lawton Challenge Cup class and 16 year old Derek Hanson took full advantage subjecting the audience, the adjudicator and Horace to Scherzo in B minor for at least 6 minutes. He also made some changes to his recital programme changing from Prelude and Fugue No 3 Bk 1 to No 17 Bach, he maintained that there had been a misprint but on checking his entry form the printed programme was correct.

Above: Little Mary Taylor has been doing well this week. On Monday she was second in her solo mime class and on Tuesday she won another solo acting class and was awarded a certificate in another class.

***Fig 36: Report from Southend Standard***

All this of course took up time that had not been allocated. When a competitor failed to turn up in a later class Horace has noted 'Hurrah! We were half an hour late!' The singers were told that the Festival audience was the most sympathetic in the world and that the great British public were not nearly so accommodating. This was perhaps just as well as Trevor Hardy, Adjudicator for some of the classes noted that the H.W.L.Hobbs Challenge Cup class for ladies of 19 years and above was ***'a miserable class with a miserable song - Madam Noy was a most difficult song with difficult rhythm and few people got it'.*** He also criticised the Choir classes as having widely differing numbers in each choir in the same class, Eastwood High School had 78 people in the choir whilst Ridley Studios Junior choir only had 20. The choirs were difficult to manage this year, Horace noted that the hall was 'packed out' with people sitting on the floor.

Mrs. Sita Lumsden had clearly got through her baptism of fire and was reappointed as Secretary in 1962. It was decided to try the accordion classes again and to reinstate dance classes; there had been none since 1957.

***Fig 37:* A young accordion player.**

A new Gilbert & Sullivan class was introduced and the clarinet class was extended to include other orchestral woodwind instruments. This extension managed to produce a class of flutes only! The dance classes were to include ballet, character or national and feature solo, duet and group dancing - in total there were 118 dance entries. Alas the accordion classes were again unsupported and so cancelled. An interesting development was a 'loaned' piano from Gilberts - no hire charge was made. This was particularly helpful as the Festival was becoming more expensive to run and there were concerns over finances. A steward who came to the attention of the Committee was Miss Hatch who apparently excelled at selling tickets, she took on the task with 'apparent enjoyment and great success!' A new band of certificate writers was also formed and certificates were now written on the spot. Another item of noted success was the fact that all the previous year's trophies and cups had been returned on time.

At this time there was a huge rise in the popularity of the recorder. It was the first instrument that children learned to play in school. The recorder classes were enormous with sometimes 20 plus children all playing the same piece. One such child was our current Honorary Secretary, Annette Forkin:

*Fig 38: Annette Forkin 1962.*

SOUTHEND MUSICAL FESTIVAL

FIRST PRIZE

AWARDED TO

Annette Richardson

FOR

Recorder Solo

CLASS No. [illegible]

David Martin

ADJUDICATOR

[illegible]

Date November [illegible]

MOZART
HAYDN
WEBER

SMF

HANDEL
CHOPIN
BRAHMS

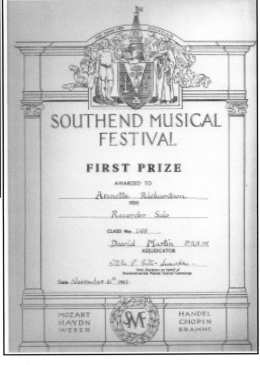

A family who between them took some of those trophies home with 12 first prizes in various classes were the Gowings - Mum, Dad, Janet and James. The youngest competitor that year was 5 year old Wendy Bright who performed in the dance class and it was noted in the press that 'lively children dominate the music festival'. Henry Isaacs, Adjudicator for piano noted that all the children ***'tried to make music rather than just play piano'***, although his opinion of the harpsichord was rather withering describing the sound as ***'playing on a birdcage with a toasting fork'.*** Peter Hearn, Adjudicator for Speech and Drama described the choral verse speaking as a 'delightful class, with tremendously exciting work'. Margaret Steward was described as a 'most attractive singer, every point made with lovely tone'. Strings and Woodwind attracted an unusual entry from Rochford Secondary School, who gave a rendition of the Theme from Z Cars arranged for recorder. The group didn't win but came second with 82 marks. The solo recorder class for 11 years and under attracted 43 entries. The 1962 Festival also saw the first entry into the competition of a young Helen Mirren, now Dame Helen Mirren, who went on to become one of the country's most acclaimed actresses. She entered the Shakespeare Cup class for 14 - 17 year olds. Whilst she did not win the cup, she did gain a highly respectable 88 marks for her recital of a passage from Henry VI.

In a bid to solve at least some of the problems of overcrowding at the prize concerts it was decided that certificates should be given at the end of a class and only prizes and trophies be awarded at the concert.

In 1963 a new class was added to speech and drama - that of British Dialect. It was also noted that an entry from a Male Voice Choir had been received after many years of absence. Things were again becoming difficult financially for the Festival, the church fees for Clifftown had increased and it was no longer available to use on a Wednesday, the parlour couldn't be used at all other than on Saturdays and for one Friday for choirs. Again the thinking caps had to go on to save money - a change of printers reduced that bill by £30, certificates written on the spot and only if requested saved a little more; entrance fees in some classes were to be increased, as were members' subscriptions.

Although entry numbers had risen to 1,369 in 1963 there was concern that a number of local teachers had retired and that new teachers were reluctant to enter their pupils in the competition. Due consideration was to be given to encouraging new teachers to support the Festival. Another suggestion was to spread the competitions over four weeks thus increasing the gate money and making the whole thing easier to organise. Although venues would again prove to be a challenge. The dance classes were held at Dowsett School but as no money could be taken at the door this meant selling entry tickets in advance.

The Festival was often the recipient of sheet music, Miss Toltman, a retired local teacher, donated her collection containing many prize winning volumes. These volumes were given to competitors 'who could ill afford to buy such music'.

The Prize Winners' Concert came in for some criticism this year, as it was felt that the standards had dropped from the Festival performance. A note was placed in the programme for 1964 reminding competitors that they were expected to maintain their standard for the concert should they win their class. There was also instruction on a dress code for the event - evening or party dress.

1964 saw the introduction of modern and tap dancing which proved very successful, but a suggestion to restart country dancing was refused. In the same year Freda Parry received more national acclaim taking part in a BBC broadcast of 'Meet the Choir', and 1964 produced the best Beethoven class for some years. Audrey Hewson ***'gave as good an interpretation as you could get from any seasoned artist, with colour and an air of confidence.'***

The Festival was also privileged to have Isobel Baillie a singer of world wide eminence adjudicate the singing classes in 1964. A Scottish soprano, Isobel enjoyed a long and illustrious career. She was renowned for her performance of the Messiah and reportedly sang it over 1000 times. She received an OBE in 1951 and was made a Dame in 1978, her advice to would be singers was simple, ‘ Never sing louder than lovely’.

**Dame Isobel Baillie**
**Her advice to singers was**
**"Never sing louder than lovely"**

***Fig 39: Dame Isobel Baillie.***

The British Dialect class attracted entries for Cockney, Welsh, Lancashire and Scottish accents, although it is not known exactly what form the classes took. In dance and drama classes the Ridley Studios dominated with several groups - the Saturday Seniors, Wednesday Intermediates, Eastwood Group and the Student Theatre Group all took part under the Ridley Studios banner.

The dress code for the Prize Winners' Concert had been observed with the press commenting that 'pretty dresses are so important for any platform performance.' There was no comment in terms of what the men were wearing!

Again, overcrowding and lengthy presentations were causing problems at the Prize Winners' Concert. For 1965 it was decided that the presentation of cups and trophies was to be made at the time of the class and then be returned for display only at the concert. The Willison Cup was subject to new rules and in the event of a tie the singers were to perform again to identify an outright winner. Other rules for the prizewinners were also introduced in 1965. Prize vouchers were to be exchanged directly with the shops no later than the 1st January 1966, also cups and shields would only be engraved at the Festival's expense until 1st January 1966, after this date any engraving was at the cost of the competitor!

Costs were again causing concern in 1966 and the issue of the cost of the adjudicators' criticisms was again raised. The entry fees for classes were to be increased to cover the costs of producing the criticism sheet. Guitars were now to be included in the strings classes and accordion classes expanded to include harmonicas.

Despite the rather frosty acceptance of a Parents Class in previous years - it lasted one year only - another attempt was made this year to involve the family as a whole in the Festival with the Home Music Making class. This class could contain any combination of voice and / or instrument within one family. The accompanist had to be of the family or the official accompanist was to be used. The Festival of 1966 had 1482 entries and Miss Hatch continued to sit in a 'howling draught selling tickets' - this will sound familiar to those of us who did the same last year!

The dance section was reported as splendid and running like clockwork. Not so the Speech and Drama, for 1967 it was decided to move these classes to the Youth Theatre. The Prize Winners' Concert saw the Mayor express the hope that the Festival could be held in the new Civic Centre. The controversy that accompanied the 1966 festival was the matter of several piano trophies and cups being won by 'outsiders', some parents complained that this was not acceptable. The Committee felt that if the 'locals' didn't approve they should 'raise their game!'

The usual review of the Festival brought about some more changes in classes for 1967 - the Women's Institute and Madrigal Choir classes appeared to be out of fashion at this time and so were dropped, and a brass section was introduced. A suggestion had been made that the Festival should combine with Leigh Festival and create one drama section per year for the district; this was refused and so the Festival now had four venues to deal with: Leigh Community Centre, Clifftown Church, the Youth Theatre and the Civic Centre.

In the event entries were down by 150 in 1967 as there had been a problem with late entries and many were refused as the programme was already at the printers and could not be changed. The strings section in particular suffered from very low entries and the Committee felt that positive canvassing in schools should start as soon as possible to encourage more entries for 1968. The Youth Theatre venue was a resounding success giving experience of a large stage with adequate wings. Peter Hearn, Adjudicator commented that it was a 'great training ground for performers and producers'. The Civic Centre however did not come up to scratch as a venue; whilst the Committee felt that 'as a representative function of Southend we should be in the Civic Centre', the stage was too small to accommodate the choirs and the atmosphere was described as 'very dry'. In addition to this poor Miss Hatch had a 'thin time in a dimly lit and very cold foyer' - howling gales are one thing but you do need to be able to see your quarry in the important matter of extracting their ticket money! Whilst the stage may have been too small nothing was to stop the Freda Parry Singers from winning the Louise Boland Challenge Cup with 'ravishing tone'.

Songs from the Shows was a new addition to the festival and produced renditions from South Pacific, Oklahoma, Oliver and the Sound of Music. Each competitor showed the 'personality and charm' required to sing show songs well. It was deemed to be an excellent and very popular class.

A source of great pride and excitment this year was the awards of MBE and OBE to Wilfred Waller and Freda Parry. The Festival finances were still causing some concern in 1968 and the year started with an overdraft of £40. The role of publicity officer was now an official post and it can be seen from the programme that the advertising revenue was increased. A wide range of local businesses and other events of musical interest in the town were now advertised amongst the pages.

***Fig 40:***
***Mr. Wilfrld Waller MBE -***

Gerald Usher now joined the Committee bringing his expertise in conducting choirs, organ playing and general musicianship. He enjoyed several successful years competing in the Festival with his school choir, Fitzwimarc. He spent a great deal of time creating the musical arrangements for the performances and still firmly believes choir training is an art. Gerald remains very much a part of the local music community, teaching both in schools and individual pupils. Whilst an accomplished musician he never wished to perform himself, being happy as an accompanist.

***Fig 41: Gerald Usher.***

***Fig 42: Pupils of Fitzwimarc School Choir, 1968.***

The 1968 Festival was a great success with 1,436 entries. The strings section enjoyed a revival and the hand bell ringing class also proved very attractive with two teams competing.

In the dance classes a new talent was to emerge - that of Marcia Gresham Jacobson. This young lady was to go on and win countless classes at the Festival over the next few years. Another dancer who subsequently followed a professional career with the Royal Ballet was Joanna Allnatt, both girls feature frequently in the lists of winners throughout the 1960s and 70s. Joanna's mother is Denise Raynsford - another great supporter of the Festival, who took the role of Secretary from 1993 - 2000 and both she and Pat Jacobson, Marcia's Mum were Convenors of the Dance Section. Both ladies are still involved with the Festival.

*Fig 43: Marcia Gresham Jacobson. 1968*

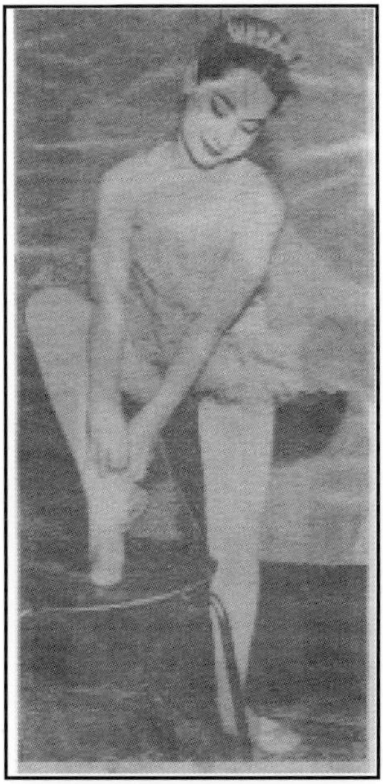

As the decade drew to a close there were some changes ahead. Mrs Sita Lumsden now took on the role of assistant Treasurer as well to see the Festival safely through to the introduction of decimal currency. Catering costs were now to be shown in the accounts as the cost was growing enough to warrant its own column! 1970 saw Mrs. Sita Lumsden resign as the Festival Secretary but she continued to support the Festival by becoming the Entries Secretary. Miss Heppel now took up the role.

It was brought to the attention of the Committee that trophies and prizes were generally disappearing from Musical Festivals and that certificates only were being awarded. Indeed many Festivals had melted down their trophies! In the centenary year we can be thankful that the Committee decided to keep all the trophies and shields associated with the Southend Musical Festival. It is safe to state that many of the shields and trophies awarded at Southend are considered to be priceless and as well as their monetary value the historical value cannot be measured. The Choir and Drama shields are coveted by local schools and others and continue to look splendid in the school trophy cabinet and be a source of inspiration and pride.

1969 was the biggest Festival on record with 1,810 competitors. There was no sign of this popular local event slowing down or disappearing as it approached its 60th Anniversary.

***Fig 44: Prizewinners 1962***

Fig 45:
Robin Truckner

years-old Robin Tickner
a pupil of St. Thomas
More School, came firs

for 11-years-old childre

Fig 46: Mary Abrahams & Rosalyn Elvin

Four pupils from Earls Hall Junior School, Prittlewell (above), run
through the piece of music which won them first prize at the Musical
Festival. They are Graham Campbell, Raymond Dix, Margaret Head-
land and Cheryl Isaacs.


Fig 47: Earls Hall Junior School.

*Figs 48 & 49: Prizewinners.*

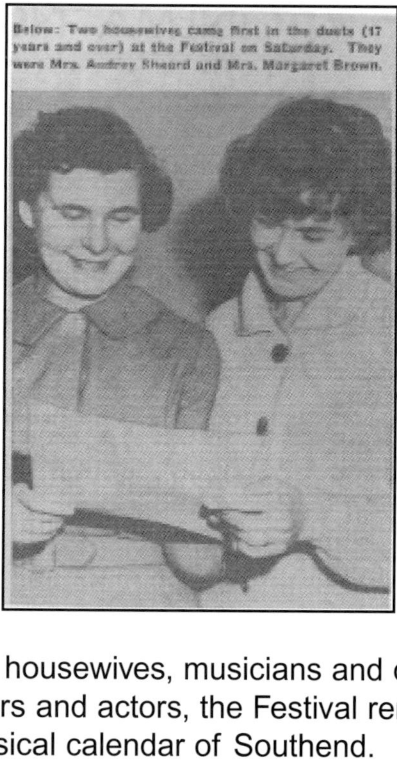
Below: Two housewives came first in the duets (17 years and over) at the Festival on Saturday. They were Mrs. Audrey Sheard and Mrs. Margaret Brown.

From children to housewives, musicians and dancers and of course the singers and actors, the Festival remained a great event on the musical calendar of Southend.

## Technology & Travesty
## 1970 - 1989.

The decades of the 70s and 80s saw an explosion of technology in every aspect of life. Household gadgets such as the microwave and colour television became commonplace, and computers started their steady infiltration into the general population. Although it is worthy of note that despite advances in technology and communication we still needed the invention of the Post-It note in 1979!

Record players and the Sony walkman transformed how we listened to music, with drum machines and synthesizers changing the way in which we played it. The Casio keyboard became a must have for the kids alongside skateboards, chopper bikes and space hoppers.

The popular music scene became even more bizarre and threatening to sensible adults as 'Glam Rock' clashed with 'Punk', giving way to 'New Romantics' and 'Hip Hop' - come back the Beatles all is forgiven! If John, Paul, George and Ringo horrified parents with the length of their hair then Boy George was definitely a step too far that included pretty make up for the boys! In amongst all the new music genres there remained the tolerable middle of the road of Abba and The Carpenters to sooth the much furrowed parental brow, and of course Kylie and Jason could always be relied upon to counteract the Sex Pistols.

Whilst some traditions were dying out during these twenty years the one that never fails in Southend is that of the pier. A fire in 1976 caused extensive damage and in 1986 it was sliced in two by the Merchant Vessel Kingsabbey!

The Festival entered the 1970s in relatively good shape. Wilfrid Waller remained Chairman and Phyllis Gayler clocked up 40 years as the official accompanist. There were various new classes - the Clulow Challenge Cup for verse speaking was to be awarded for the first time. Also in 1970 a new prose speaking class was included where competitors had to choose a newspaper article from any date and present it. The Horace

Bayliss Cup was also to be awarded in 1970 in a new class for any voice, 18 years and over with an 'own choice' song. There were 23 entries for this class. The cash prize for the best performance of a Selim Palmgen work was withdrawn as there were no entries and the sponsor did not want to allocate the prize to another class. Palmgen, whilst not necessarily a household name, was a Finnish composer, pianist and conductor. He enjoyed a very successful career both in Finland and the USA. His opera 'Daniel Hjort' was first performed in 1910.

The Festival of 1970 reached the highest number of entries to date giving over 2000 performances. The standards remained very high and some 75% of performers achieved certificates. This was somewhat frowned upon as being very expensive and, in some cases, wasteful as some were not collected. However, overall the Festival was once again a great success. The woodwind and brass section was noted to practically run itself with teachers and competitors being old friends meeting at the Festival year after year in the 'friendliest of rivalries.' There was concern once more over 'outsiders' taking trophies, Beal Grammar School for Girls from Ilford swept up no less than 7 awards in the Choir classes. The 8 ladies from Buttsbury - all over 65 years of age - didn't win but were worthy of a mention in the minutes as entertaining. There was renewed interest in the Choir classes this year with entries from 2 women's institute choirs and 3 from various townswomen's guild choirs. The dance section was devoid of any classes for boys this year although one or two determined lads did put in performances in the duet classes and some competed against the girls in the tap and modern dance classes. The Lale family entered the Home Music Making class as an ensemble and were successful. As individuals they also entered several other classes with success - another thoroughly musical family. The orchestral class was won by the Fitzwimarc School under the watchful eye of Gerald Usher.

For the first time a scholarship class appeared in the

syllabus having been discussed and rejected in previous years. The Ridley Studios offered a one year training programme to anyone under 10 years who had not had any formal speech and drama lessons.

Despite the large number of entries to the Festival the balance in hand at the end of 1970 was £69 12s 3d and with increased postal charges, telephone and venue costs to contend with the cost cutting caps were duly doffed once more. There was also the issue of the restoration of the grand piano at Clifftown Church Hall. A promise had been made to make a donation to this fund and the treasurer stated that we could only afford £5. The Executive Committee had felt a sum of £25 would be more appropriate, even though the Festival only made use of the piano for 8 days per year. The matter was settled at the next meeting and a donation of £10 was made.

Cost cutting measures this time around were to include sending entry slips to teachers en masse for them to distribute to their pupils rather than individual postage to competitors. Entry fees were also to be increased by 5p (decimalisation had arrived!) - whilst 5p sounds very little, in real terms this equalled one old shilling - quite a rise in the entry fee. The syllabus was to be 'pruned' to save on printing costs and hand delivered where possible, and the admission price for the public was also to increase. Although the stalwart Miss Hatch had retired so renewed vigilance would be required if the higher fee was to be collected.

Sadly, 1971 got off to a shocking start with the death of Madam Freda Parry OBE in January. A longstanding supporter of the Festival, and musical legend in the town, the minutes note that the 'whole Festival body has lost one of its dearest friends'. This was the 60th year anniversary for the Festival and a Grand Concert of Prizewinners was held with the proceeds going to the Freda Parry Memorial Fund. The report for 1971 records the Speech and Drama Adjudicator testing the younger candidates on their understanding of the words they were speaking - quite a few did not understand at all, leaving the adjudicator less than impressed. The singers were reminded that they had a responsibility not just to the composer of the songs but to the poet of the lyrics also, and the pianists carried off the Senior Beethoven class on a 'note of triumph'.

***Fig 50: Madam Freda Parry OBE, 1939***

The Lale family continued to enjoy success in various classes and Marcia Gresham-Jacobson not only continued her domination of the dance classes - taking the Allnatt Challenge Cup and the Jane Rosenthal Memorial Cup but also achieving top marks of 90 in the duologue class partnering Stephen Meredith. Following the death of Freda Parry, The Parry Choir was renamed, at her request, as The Parry Singers and continued to perform at the festival with a new conductress - Edna Sewell.

Cash flow remained an issue for the Festival and the next stage of cutting the costs reveals just how hard times were - the adjudicators helpers had up to this point enjoyed free tea and biscuits - this was brought to an end and from 1972 a 5p charge would be made for each refreshment!

The Festival itself again reached over 2000 entries and the piano classes in particular were given extremely high praise. The Adjudicator was Mr. Guy Johnston who called the Chopin class ***'a tour de force - of a high standard rarely heard by adjudicators'*** and once again the Senior Beethoven class achieved ***'a monumental performance - the finest I have heard in 30 years!'.*** Catherine L. Marwood achieved a mark of 100% for her recorder solo.

## Cathy's a world-beater

RECORDER-playing schoolgirl Catherine Marwood has astounded a leading world expert on the recorder. She played an item in Southend Music Festival better than the Dutch master who made it famous.

And that was how Dr. Walter Bergmann came to award 14-year-old Catherine a maximum hundred marks for her solo performance — the first time a full 100 points had been given in the festival history.

But it wasn't Catherine's only success. She also had 98 points in the descant or treble recorder solo at the festival which has just ended.

Music is quite a family affair in the Marwood family from Roxwell Road, Chelmsford. Sister Caroline, 16, was placed second in the woodwind solo at the Festival, and, together with Catherine and brother Christopher, 10, won the recorder consort section.

Catherine is a member of the National Youth Orchestra where she plays the viola and she is studying for a musical career.

● Results — Page 11.

***Fig 51: Evening Echo Nov 1972***

Horace Bayliss passed away in 1972. There is no doubt that he left an astounding legacy of a musical community behind him. He also must have felt extremely gratified to have seen the festival continue and flourish in its 60 years, 58 of which he had been involved with. The role of Honorary Adviser to the Festival died with Horace and the executive meeting of March 1973 held a minutes silence. As the Chairman noted, 'no one else connected with the festival had his special knowledge.' Perhaps the true measure of his contribution lies in the fact that the

Festival has continued into its centenary year with the basic principles set out in 1911 remaining the same.

Phyllis Gayler, another longstanding member of the Executive Committee and the official accompanist for 40 years requested an assistant, 'preferably under the age of 30 years to gain experience in the role'. Throughout the Festival history the official accompanist was granted an honorarium in payment for her services.

The Evening Echo newspaper sent along two reporters to the Festival in 1972 and each wrote an article about their experiences. Maureen Dykes didn't get off to a very good start. She arrived after the beginning of the Bible Reading class and found herself wrestling with a door that just did not seem to want to open up and let her in. When she finally got the door open it was to find an elderly gentleman steward on the other side clutching what was left of his green ribbon to prevent late entries to the hall! All door stewards have similar experiences on an hourly basis throughout the Festival! On reading her account of the visit you could be forgiven for assuming that she and her colleague were playing 'good cop / bad cop'. Alternatively, Graham Fitzgerald appears to have a more positive view. The two very different articles appear below:

Mr. Charles Baron, aged 54, gave an astonishing performance on his violin. He had travelled from Grimsby to compete in the Festival and also to achieve a life long ambition of playing in public. He had given up his job as an accountant to study the violin and his teachers had urged him to enter the competition. His performance was judged as 'good enough to be professional, and too good for the Festival', therefore the judges thanked him and praised him but ruled him out of the competition! There was also the matter of being an adult and competing against children - his wife commented that it had been 'marvellous practice' for him anyhow.

Although entries reached over 2000 again in 1973 there is very little coverage of the festival in the local press, apparently due to a strike by reporters.

# I didn't get off to a very good start

**says Maureen Dykes**

MY VISIT to Southend Music Festival did not get off to too good a start. I could not open the door into Cliftown Memorial Hall so I gave it a hefty push. The door flew open and with it, out came a poor gentleman who had been hanging on to a piece of green string attached to the other side.

He was holding on to it to stop people from marching midway through items. He was left with six inches of fraying string in his hand.

It might have been an hilarious adjunct to a night at the local thespians — but in the hallowed sanctity of a church hall and a music festival it was all a little irreverent on my behalf. Especially as the class in progress was Bible reading.

The first thing that struck me were all the official notices stuck around the oak-panelled hall. No Smoking. Silence. Mind the Steps. No one would dare to smoke, surely. And the silence was most certainly golden, while the speech of the youngsters was of gleaming silver, highly polished for the event.

So nicely spoken for the Bible reading and verse speaking classes. They were so charming. Did they talk like that in the playground at school?

If butter would not melt in their mouths, it was the sort of occasion when one felt the need of a lozenge to melt on the tongue. A sore throat, a tickle in the tonsils. But who'd dare cough?

To me, the whole thing seemed a dreadful ordeal. The entrants had to wait in the wings — at the foot of the stairs until they went on stage. But they didn't seem too perturbed. Apart from the adjudicator, the audience itself was hyper-critical. All those who had done their readings sat and listened.

The silence during each reading was almost claustrophobic. Mothers nodded approvingly and at the end the polite applause, while other competitors got their heads together to discuss the performance.

One or two appeared to be over-doing it a bit. The adjudicator pointed out the dangers of going "over the top." On the whole, the adjudication was ultra-fair and generous and the marking very close indeed.

The verse speaking had a choice of poems — Rocket to the Moon by local poet Douglas Gibson or The Way Through The Woods by Rudyard Kipling. Most chose the Kipling piece. And here of course, reciting without the book, there was scope for a few more mistakes.

One little lad forgot to give the title of his poem. Three little girls in the front row turned round to a friend behind and said: "Um, he forgot the title."

Another poor little girl forgot the words. It produced a shiver of embarrassment from me. If only the stage could swallow the poor girl up. She was prompted by the adjudicator a couple of times, while the [illegible] three in front sniggered and giggled behind their hands.

Another clever girl sat next to me mouthing the lines with great expertise. The forgetful one left the stage, beetroot red with her hands clapped over her face. She didn't cry though, she burst into fits of giggles.

All those weeks, months of preparation. I left thinking of a homily imparted to me by a teacher at school — it seemed [illegible] true too: "Some poets are difficult, but Kipling is ruddy hard."

# It's not the winning but the taking part

**by Graham Fitzgerald**

[illegible]

which the strings and piano section was well under way.

The halls on the small side and there were something like 100 things, about half of them filled, mainly by competitors with a few parents.

The first thing to strike one was the air of informality and general enjoyment — even on the faces of performers.

Obviously, [illegible] a [illegible] experience for them, a far cry from examinations when the entrants sit huddled, usually in unsociable waiting rooms, looking nervous and apprehensive.

One reason for this is that there was no pass mark, so no-one was facing the ghastly prospect of failure.

The other, and main one, was, I think, the warm and kind way that judge Miss Norah Jamieson — who incidentally adjudicated at the Leigh Music Festival earlier this year — was discharging her duties.

She gave the impression that she had all the time in the world and that every competitor, regardless of their standard, was of equal importance.

They were allowed as much time as they wanted to prepare themselves and on two occasions when competitors suggested that they make a second start or go back a few bars, they were allowed to do so without comment.

When it came to awarding marks she was perhaps a trifle over-generous but only a little. I hear learn that one young man was given 100 out of 100; well, no one is worth that!

What impressed most was her comments. They weren't only addressed to the individual concerned but to everyone present and she frequently called people out to the floor to demonstrate what she meant.

I, for one, learnt a tremendous amount, and Gerald Usher, Southend's music chief who was sitting next to me, said he did too.

She drew attention to bow action, the fact that the bow should be at an angle of 90 degrees to the string, that not too much action should come from the elbow, that one should keep one's eye on the music and so on. Every hand, all these points explained with perfect clarity.

In every way Miss Jamieson was a model judge and I sincerely hope that Southend will have the sense to ask her back.

The organisation was excellent, with a small group of women seated on the left of the performing area making sure that everything ran smoothly.

The number of the class was put up on a sizeable board so that one had no difficulty following events.

Among the classes I heard were Nos. 111, duet for two violins with piano accompaniment (age 16 years and under), 101, concerto class for violin or viola (open) and 100, violin solo (open).

Generally, the standard was extremely high and among the works performed were the opening movement from Walton's Viola Concerto, the last movement of Vivaldi's Violin Concerto in A Minor, Op. 3 No. 6 and Lalo's *Symphonie Espagnole*.

Here came an excellent example of the judge's fairness. Miss Jamieson described the performer, 14-year-old Mr. Charles Baron, as being in "a different class" from the rest.

"Are you a professional?" she asked him. No. "Then you very nearly are. I don't propose to award you a mark; merely to thank you for playing to us."

Mr. Baron didn't think his performance merited such praise (and neither did I), and was shaking his head violently. But Miss Jamieson's opinion was unquestionably the right one.

*Figs 52 & 53: Evening Echo November 1972.*

1974 gave the Festival a new Chairman as Wilfrid Waller retired after 18 years. Bernard Birn now took up the post. There were some other changes to the Committee as Gerald Usher took up post as Musical Director to Essex Authority and stepped down as Convenor for the strings section. Mrs Horace Bayliss and Mr & Mrs Wilfrid Waller were made Honorary Members for their long and loyal service.

Money was again a problem, the cost of using Clifftown Hall was to increase by 50%. To try and offset this entry fees and subscriptions were again to be increased. Postage was also to be carefully monitored as the price of a first class stamp was now 4 1/2p! The Prize Winners Concert was also reduced once more to 3 concerts rather than 4.

1974 saw a large reduction in entries to the Festival at 1847 and 33 of the classes had no entries at all. The Prize Winners Concert became the usual headache made worse by the fact that if competitors received their prizes of cash or book vouchers at the time of the class they were less likely to attend the concert. The solution was to give a voucher that indicated the value of the prize but the prize itself was to be awarded at the prizewinners concert. This ploy still left £13 worth of vouchers unclaimed in 1975.

The longstanding arrangement with the Clifftown Hall came to an end in 1975 and the venue for the Festival was to be the Civic Centre Assembly Hall. Dancing was to continue at Leigh Community Centre and the Executive meetings were now to be held at the library. A 4th Prize Winners Concert was to be held once more, this time the dance section got a Prize Winners Concert of its own.

After careful consideration in 1976 the over 60s got a class of their own, noted in the minutes is the comment ‘ we shall, without doubt, be surprised to see how young at heart they are.’ This class did indeed prove to be popular and remains so.

The next few years the Festival continued as per usual with money continuing to be a cause of concern. A substantial personal donation by the Entries Secretary was made 'that should and must set it in its feet once more financially'.

Sheila Heppel, the Honorary Secretary for the last 8 years, stepped down in 1977 and Rita Ellis now took on the job. A further donation of £50 now placed the Festival in credit and a 'money saving' committee was formed to attempt to keep the finances on track. The Musical Council became the 'Friends of the Festival' with subscriptions of £2.00 per 'friend'. It was also decided that 32 pages could be removed from the syllabus giving a substantial saving on the printing costs. Something must have been working as the 1977 Festival saw a profit of £367.00! This was also a celebratory year for the Queens Silver Jubilee and a special trophy was awarded for the most outstanding performance of the festival. Sadly, the programme held in the archives does not note the winner.

With finances looking less difficult there were several other financial bonuses in 1978. A 50% reduction in the hire fee for the Civic Centre Monday - Thursday and a very generous anonymous benefactor gave a donation of £5000, which was invested to provide interest income. It seemed as though the financial crisis of previous years could now be avoided in the future. Charitable status was also to be sought. This would give the Festival the advantage of tax free interest and various waivers of other charges that would help maintain the now healthy financial state and provide security for future Festivals.

Now that cash was not such a worry, attention became more focused on the running of the Festival itself and the minutes start to reflect discussion on matters such as identity badges for Festival Officials, how to cut down the noise from children in the waiting rooms and who should tune stringed instruments. An interval for tea and coffee between sessions was agreed along with a reduction in fees for multiple entries - a sort of enter 4 classes and get one free system!

FDL Penny, a Festival supporter since 1921, had passed away in 1977 and had left a legacy of a scholarship class for an instrumentalist aged 14 - 18 years. The prize was £50 and was to be used to further the winners musical studies. It also came with the opportunity to play with the King Edmund Sinfonia. The class was restricted to entrants living in Southend, Rochford or Castle Point and they had to perform 2 solo pieces of their own choice but of contrasting styles. David Lale won the first scholarship for this class playing Cello. The prize was to be rotated through different disciplines each year.

The report on the 1978 Festival shows it as being one of the most successful for many years. The overall profit was £356 meaning that the interest from the anonymous donation did not need to be used. It was however a bit of a shock to find out that the Festival had to pay 42% corporation tax on the interest generated. Charitable status had not yet been achieved, to qualify as a charity we needed a constitution. It was also decided that we needed our own piano stools as relying on chairs for performers was not satisfactory! There was also some discussion about insuring the cups and trophies, whilst there was insurance it was far too low to cover the replacement of the items . The shields and cups were fast approaching the realms of being priceless in terms of history.

Phyllis Gayler announced that 1979 was to be her last year as the official accompanist. She had now been in post for 50 years! Stella Sita-Lumsden and Sir Stephen McAdden, President of the Festival, both died in 1979. Stella had held the post of Secretary for several years.

Our current President, Sir Teddy Taylor, was invited to the post in 1979 and accepted. Throughout the 1970s several now well known local musicians and dramatists started their competitive careers - Liz Elliot, Ann Barber and Rosemary Pennington among others continue to work in the local musical community.

The 1970s saw some key events in the history of the country concluding with the winter of discontent in 1979 as miners, postal workers and dustmen went on strike. The 1980s was to be the decade of decadence, Mrs. Thatcher, yuppies and the fall of the Berlin Wall. 1984 was the year of Band Aid for the famine in Ethiopia, 1985 gave us the first episode of Eastenders - the cast of which has been known to have the odd day trip to Saarfend and also includes a former competitor in Kara Tointon - and Michael Jackson's Thriller album sold 20 million copies.

The eighties decade started out with a look at the rules for choirs. The concerns centred around previous contact, including coaching, with the Adjudicators. The Parry Singers wrote to the Committee suggesting that any competitor who had received coaching or had any other form of contact with the Adjudicator in the preceding three years should not be eligible to enter. A warning was issued in the syllabus to that effect but the time limit was reduced to one year.

The Civic Centre was not available for the Festival of 1981 so it was held between Leigh Community Centre and the Youth Theatre, both together were cheaper than the Civic Centre. There were difficulties with the Community Centre as it could only house 192 people and all had to be seated due to fire regulations. When including competitors and stewards this severely limited the capacity for the public to attend. Also the dancing and singing license stipulated that performances could not start before 10.00am. The whole day needed to be booked for the Prize Winners Concert to allow for the delivery and tuning of the piano. It was also imperative to ensure that the caretaker was notified of this arrangement, the previous year the piano and the tuner had a long wait outside whilst someone was found to open up! In an echo of days long gone the Committee again started to wonder why there was not a decent arts centre in Southend!

In 1981 a draft constitution was put forward for consideration of charitable status. This was a slow process and was not granted to the Festival until 1982.

Entries were considerably lower than in 1980 as one of the main dance schools in the area did not enter any pupils. This led to a reduction of 400 entries. There were as usual a few gems in terms of performance. The dance Adjudicator called for an encore from Maxine Smith and Amanda Bell, both

13 years old, who reportedly 'brought the house down' with their comedy duet.

Not all the reports were positive. For the first time in the Festival history there was a mountain of bad publicity, in the past there had been constructive criticism of the Festival, but in general all press had been very positive and supportive. This shocking development could be attributed to one man - the villain of the piece was a certain Lionel Salter, Adjudicator.

He managed to upset various competitors and at one point a whole orchestra were left in tears as he pronounced their efforts to play were 'unadulterated rubbish!'. When challenged about his manner he remained unrepentant - 'If the music is rubbish I will say so... that Tchaikovsky interpretation was a thoroughly tasteless distortion.' One teacher remarked that whilst he was capable of good marking and good adjudication he clearly had bad manners! It was noted that 'old stagers' will find little new in this level of criticism, but teachers and parents alike were disgusted that little children had been left crying.

***Fig 54: Lionel Salter Adjudicator.***

On a happier note the story of an exceedingly ancient gentleman who competed each year was reported, giving some balance. This gentleman had become somewhat of an embarrassment to the adjudicators who could not actually award him a prize and hardly any marks, his voice had faded so badly over time. However, he clearly thoroughly enjoyed taking part - at the start of his performance he would twirl around and with his back to the audience would expertly remove his false teeth - a worthy start to the class!

Since 1911 the Festival has witnessed many personal triumphs, disasters and dramas, one could argue that this is what the Festival is about.

In 1982 it was decided not to hold the Prize Winners Concert. The Committee felt that it was not worth it financially, it took a great deal to organise and produced very little in terms of profit. The 1983 minutes note that no one seemed to miss it! Entries were once again topping 2000 and the press gave very good coverage.

***Fig 55: Festival pictures.***

Alice Oates pictured below, first won a book in a piano class at the festival in 1911. In 1983 she won a cup in the composition class!

Accommodating the Festival was once again an issue as the community centre had proved to be too small for the last night of the dancing classes and people were turned away. It was decided that the Trinity Methodist Hall would now be its new home. This however brought its own problems as some

Alice, 88 is still in love with festival

LIKE THIS: Alice and members of the Hockley Singing Group go through her composition.

***Figs 56 & 57:***

***Alice Oates.***

singers withdrew from the competition after objecting to performing secular songs, such as those from the shows or traditional folk songs, in a church. This remains an issue and although secular songs are performed within the church venue attention is always given to the lyrics and any potential offence that could be caused. If songs chosen by competitors are not felt to be appropriate they are asked to either modify the lyric or change the song.

1983 saw further controversy in the Speech and Drama section. Complaints were received about obscene language used in some of the classes. Whilst some modern drama did contain swear words it was felt that this was inappropriate for a a competitive festival and there were often young children present in the audience. A letter was sent to the teachers asking that they consider this when choosing pieces for their pupils. The result was a drop in entries in 1984 'due to the executive decision on the use of controversial language.' The Festival made a loss of £625!

Platform manners were again a subject of debate - performers should bow to the audience before leaving the stage and soloists should acknowledge the accompanist - were two of the points raised, along with the ever annoying question of suitable attire!

1985 brought the death of Winifred Nancarrow. She was a longstanding member of the Committee and musical community.

Money matters being on the agenda once more it was with some relief that the Committee welcomed Paul Airey to join its ranks as a co-opted member. He was instrumental in obtaining sponsorship for the Festival from local businesses and donated the piano for free. He also made attempts for prizewinners to perform live on Essex radio, although these did not come to fruition. Paul became an active member of the Committee, promoting the Festival wherever he could.

There were no dance classes in 1985 due to a lack of support from the local dance schools and it was expected that this would result in a large monetary loss. As it happened the Festival made a profit that year of £340.49, added to the interest income the Festival had a healthy £1200 balance in hand. Although the cost of hiring halls was still very much an issue.

The dance classes returned in 1986 but were limited to one week with a separate program. It was also the 75th Anniversary year for the festival. A luncheon to celebrate this achievement was hosted by Sir Teddy Taylor.

AFTER THREE: Bobby Birn and Dorothy Havis at the piano with, left to right, Eileen Greaves, Mr Taylor, Joyce Birn, Mr Bayliss, Mrs Collard, Donald Collard and John Curtis


***Fig 58: 75th Anniversary Lunch. Back L to R: Eileen Greaves (Hon Sec); Sir Teddy Taylor (President); Joyce Birn; Peter Bayliss; Louise Collard; Don Collard; John Curtis. Bobby Birn & Dorothy Havis at the piano.***

There was another source of income that the Committee could consider - that of selling off some of the trophies. Other Festivals had done this over the years but once again we were not going to follow the trend! The Festival managed to make a profit in 1986 and overall the accounts were reported to show 'a very satisfactory state of affairs'.

There was some debate about whether cash prizes were appropriate or in the spirit of the Festival, the Federation frowned upon them feeling that they introduced an 'unworthy element' to the proceedings. The committee decided to continue with them, they totalled some £227.00 overall.

There were also concerns over competitors leaving the hall following their class and not staying for the whole session, one member noted that ***'there is a general lack of interest, it's a fact of life, people have lost the art of listening and concentration.'***

In 1988 consideration was given to changing the marking system once again. The question centred around whether marks should be abandoned altogether in favour of a grading system. It was felt by some of the Committee and Convenors that low marks were offputting to competitors. However no marks at all would lose the competitive element. The clue is held in the title of the Festival - COMPETITIVE! Low marks should be taken in the spirit of competition and used as a spur to improve. Some Festivals had stopped giving marks to the younger competitors as a compromise. The committee decided by a majority to keep the current system.

All classes were now open to anyone across the British Isles excluding the Penny Memorial Prize - this one class remained restricted to local entrants only. Another feather in the cap for the Festival was the news that it was to host the heats of the Southend Young Musician of the Year Competition - all expenses would be covered by the local council. Competitors were to be under 19 years, at no less than grade 7 standard and were to give a 10 minute recital.

1988 was also memorable for two of the 2011 Committee members. Liz Elliott won the Penny Memorial Prize of £50 with 90 marks for her performance of the Letter Aria from Werther by Massenet and Jena Pang made his debut in verse speaking and piano classes coming a very respectable 2nd at the age of 9 years old with 87 marks.It does appear that once bitten by the Festival bug one tends to stick with it for a lifetime!

In 1938 Dorothy West had won the Mrs. Stevens Junior Challenge Cup playing 'The Puppet's Complaint' by Franck. Some 50 years later in 1988 she presented the cup and a special prize to the winner of the class who had played the same piece. This was Tobie Abel, who won with 87 marks.

There is little information in the archives or the press cutting regarding 1989. Overall the Festival had enjoyed another successful decade. Entries had fallen from the 2000 plus high to a regular lower level of around 1500 and dance classes were substantially lower, with no dance class at all in 1986, but despite this the Committee was as committed as ever to continuing to produce one of the longest running Festivals in the country.

Times may have changed dramatically since 1911 but the basic standards and ethics of the Festival remained the same. It was a place to strive for excellence, gain experience and to test out your talents. Sir Walford Davies noted in 1985:

***'The aim is not to gain a prize or defeat a rival but to pace one another on the road to perfection.'***

## Grunge & Garage:
## 1990 - 1999.

The 1990s, as with all other decades, brought diverse changes to the world. In the early years of the decade there were many 'firsts' for the female of the species - a female head of MI5, a female Speaker in the House of Commons, a British woman in space and the introduction of women priests to the Church of England.

There was progress in the fight for freedom with the release of Nelson Mandela from prison after 27 years and the Soviet Union dissolved giving 15 separate republics independence. Also Brian Keenan, John McCarthy and Terry Waite were all released from their captivity. That was some of the good news.

In Britain the Poll Tax riots were causing a headache for government and there was an earthquake of 5.1 on the Richter scale that was felt throughout Shropshire. Not to mention heavy snowfall that - as we have now come to expect - saw the country grind to a halt.

The popular music scene contained grunge and garage music for those sturdy enough, giving way to house, techno and rave by the end of the decade. All was not lost for those who had absolutely no idea about any of it - mainly anyone over 25 and that included all of the Executive Committee - for contemporary country music arrived along with the rise of the power ballad, boy bands and Spice Girls. If all else failed there was the craze for line dancing that countered both the music and the headbanging jumping up and down that passed for dancing!

In Southend plans were being made for the celebration of the centenary of Borough status and by the end of the decade the town had become a Unitary Authority. The local music scene saw the start of the Leigh Folk Festival, still popular today and Bernard (Bobby) Birn MBE was made a Freeman of the Town for his services to music and art. A slightly bizarre record was set by Southend Girls Choir when they entered the Guiness

Book of Records for the highest altitude performance! The Southend Girls' Choir holds the world record, as verified by the Guiness Book of Records, for performing a concert at the highest altitude in an aeroplane, above the northern coast of Australia. The choir gave a 45 minute recital at a height of 36,000 feet, thus becoming the world record holders for such an event.

***Fig 59: Southend Girl's Choir.***

Just in case you were wondering I can confirm that the pier caught fire in 1995!

In terms of Southend Musical Festival the only spice that was really, really wanted was business as usual with talented people performing and competing, playing their own instruments without the aid of a computer. It wasn't that computers weren't viewed as helpful, indeed the 1990s was the decade where the organisational and administrative activities of the Festival were computerised, but lines need to be drawn and technology was to be limited to the consideration of a keyboard class.

Another new class considered in 1990 was that of

Juggling. There were to be two classes, one junior and one senior and they were to be placed within the Speech & Drama section. Keyboard classes were rejected as it was felt that they would be too complicated to set up.

Prize Winners' Concerts were also to be shelved for the time being as there had been little interest in them. The problem of venues remained and Trinity Church and the Civic Centre were booked for 1990 with Crowstone Church booked for the Choral classes in 1991. The usual rumours of an Arts Centre for the town continued to circulate and the Committee wrote to the council supporting such a project - to no avail as there was no financial provision in the council budget for an Arts Centre.

The Committee were approached by the Prayer Book Society in 1990 to hold a class for the 500th anniversary of the birth of Thomas Cranmer, a leader of the English Reformation and Archbishop of Canterbury during the reigns of Henry VIII and Edward VI. The class was for the under 16 years age group and competitors had to give readings from the 1662 Book of Common Prayer. The winner would go on to compete in a national competition. This class was agreed in principle and it was to be held at St. Saviour's Church.

1990 produced another successful Festival, entries increased in all sections. One young lady to come to the forefront of the trophy winning was Elspeth Wilkes, taking four of the senior cups - The Vera Grand Challenge Cup, the M. Lawton Challenge Cup, the Clementi Music for Pleasure Trophy and the F.D.L. Penny Memorial Prize. Elspeth had been competing at the Festival for several years.

Elspeth has enjoyed a highly successful career in music as an accompanist, teacher and musical director, specialising in opera. The Festival eventually turned into a family affair as Sandra, Elspeth's Mum started competing in the singing classes with her daughter accompanying her.

*Fig 60: Elspeth Wilkes: Growing up with the Festival.*

Whilst successful the Festival still made a loss of £550 in 1990, although this was covered by the Charity Commission Investment Account (interest of 10.3%!). More sponsors were needed, especially as 1991 was the 80th anniversary of the Festival and a special allocation of £50 prize money per section was being made. A new venue was chosen as well as a new Honorary Secretary, this task now fell to Denise Raynsford as Eileen Greaves stepped down.

The new home for the Festival was to be Highlands Church - the only proviso was that if any funerals were booked the Festival would have to vacate the premises for an hour!

The 1991 Festival was reported as very well received, the venue was bright and comfortable and there were no parking problems and thankfully no funerals!

Sadly, for such a special year there are no reports in the archives. There are some notable classes such as the Concert Band class and one extremely talented pianist in Joanna Smith who won no less than 6 trophies. She won the Southend Young Musician of the Year and eventually became the official accompanist for the Festival. A familiar name in the programme for 1991 is Jodie Marsh, who took part in the under 7's piano solo class, winning the Bronze medal with 87 marks.

Laura Burns, a highly accomplished soprano and regular competitor also made her debut in 1991, winning the F.D.L. Penny award for her performance of Madame Noy - a piece that did not win any favour with adjudicators in earlier years but one she clearly gave a stunning rendition of. The Song Recital class was won by Hilary Pell, again a very popular local mezzo-soprano who continues to perform. She also conducts the St. Bernard's School choir.

There were some organisational changes made following the Festival, one of which was that each section was now to arrange for its own stewards and the post of Chief Steward was created. The Annual General Meeting for 1992 comments on the exceptional performance of a choir of gospel singers from the Peniel Academy on the last night of the Festival. The AGM also reported the deaths of Bobby Birn, Ivy Morton-Maskell and Phyllis Gayler.

In the interests of cost cutting, thought was given to how to accommodate the adjudicators for the Festival. In the interests of the pitfalls of taking the minutes the following is an extract from the minutes of the meeting held on the 1st October 1992:

> ***'There would be a saving of £10 per day on hotel accommodation for adjudicators who were being entertained by some of the Highlands ladies....'***

Light was shed on this statement at the next meeting in December... the ladies were providing bed & breakfast for £20 per night including a light evening meal! Although all the adjudicators were very happy with their accommodation that year it was felt that hotel accommodation was indeed more appropriate.

The Festival was again popular in 1992 and 'all the children behaved beautifully' but it was time to have a hard look at the content of the Festival. There had been 80 classes with only one entry and this quite clearly could not be viewed as financially viable. However there was lengthy debate about whether such classes should be withdrawn. The view was that it would be 'artistically and educationally wrong to abolish such classes', people competed against a standard not simply against others. A decision to contact competitors and ask if they wished to withdraw from the class or continue was made.

Problems with accommodating choirs continued and it was decided to limit the size of choirs to 50 to avoid falling foul of the fire regulations and the disappointment when the hall was full to capacity and supporters could not gain admission. There was also a small matter of one choir delivering a sermon prior to the performance! The decision to limit the size of choirs caused some consternation with the singing section declaring that they would rather abandon the Freda Parry Rose Bowl award than limit the choirs who could compete for it.

Speech & Drama found itself in trouble once again with the content of a piece. This time a performer who had been successful in other classes delivered a performance that was 'crude and blasphemous and particularly outrageous when it was delivered in a church'. Whilst the adjudicator did not react strongly, a notice was to be put into the syllabus that content would now be taken into account in the marking of the performance. Another problem that needed to be solved was that of over-running. Not only was this unfair to other competitors it completely ruined the very tight schedule of the classes. It was agreed that the adjudicator would have a stop watch and that over runs would be penalised in the marking.

It was around this time that a new theatre group began to compete in the Festival. The Basildon Youth Theatre (BYT) had been homeless for a while and found little opportunity to compete. On entering the Festival they found a stage and a competitor in the Focus Theatre Group. Although their first year of competing was not a great success the group took away the Adjudicator's advice and came back the following year to win every class they entered. The rivalry between the two groups grew into a healthy respect and in some classes even collaboration. The Director of BYT, Lesley Williams pays a lovely tribute to the performers and the Festival in Chapter 8.

By this time the Festival owned an astonishing and valuable range of trophies and cups. It was suggested that they should be photographed and catalogued for identification purposes, also that winners should sign for them, undertaking to include them on their own insurance for the year. The Freda Parry bowl was estimated to be worth in excess of £2,500 at this time - not something one would want to see mislaid, notwithstanding its very special and priceless historical value. A computer would be of great benefit - if only anyone knew how to use one! It was reported that the secretary of the Ipswich Musical Festival would be visiting Southend later that year as a competitor and had agreed to bring the laptop computer that he used for Festival work and demonstrate how it could be used for producing the syllabus, programmes, criticism sheets and tickets.

Performing rights compliance is a legal requirement for the Festival and a new entry form was needed to comply with the additional information required in relation to own choice material. There was also the copyright fees for Speech & Drama material, potentially this could be very costly. Although there was an argument that the Festival was educational and should therefore be able to use such material in the same way as schools, there was no getting around the public performance part of it. A fixed contribution of £32 per annum was made based on the size of the Festival. This was affordable as at last 1992 saw a profit of £380!

There had been 230 classes in all and an extra day was needed to accommodate all of the Speech & Drama section. The musical sections were reported as showing ‘evidence that South East Essex holds future generations of musical marvels’. Three such musical marvels were found in the recorder playing of the Elman sisters - Alison, Caroline and Georgina. These girls continued to compete over several years. The Southend Junior Cooperative Choir performed two songs in Spanish to take the Gayler Trophy with 95 marks. Denise Raynsford commented that 'the children behaved splendidly and it has been a place of peace and calm'.

1993 again showed an increase in entries with 3 short of 1600. The Songs from the Shows section proved especially popular with 52 entries in the junior class and 40 in the senior. Shara Thornton won first prize of £10 for her performance of 'At the Ballet' from A Chorus Line. She did particularly well as she had been in the Accident & Emergency Department until 2 am that morning with an elbow injury.

***Fig 61: Elman sisters.***

***Fig 62: Shara Thornton.***

PROUD: Timothy Holland, centre, who came first in the verse speaking for eight-year-olds with Salwa Malik who came second and Luke Stillwell third

***Fig 63: Prize Winners.***

Sally Noble was the adjudicator for the Speech & Drama section and was particularly impressed with the choral speaking of Crowstone Preparatory School stating that they had delivered 'the best piece of group speaking I have heard in years.' She was also impressed with the overall standard of all competitors in the section saying that they had been 'sensitively taught and good communicators'.

Kara Tointon also made her first appearance at the Festival in 1992, winning the Verse Speaking class for 9 year olds with 87 marks.

The strings section was also well supported this year with 20 cello players! Southend Boys Junior Choir won the Olive Owers Cup.

This Festival generated two complaints about the adjudicators. A letter was received criticising the whole of the recorder sessions as lacking atmosphere and showing poor adjudication. The minutes simply state that this was 'not justified'. A further letter complaining that an adjudicator had publicly singled out two small boys from a school choir for bad behaviour was forwarded to the adjudicator for her comments - she replied that she had felt totally justified in telling these boys off publicly. Unlike Mr. Salter's comments these did not get reported in the media. It was decided to try a 'suggestions box' at the next Festival - when examined after the Festival in 1994 it had yielded some suggestions, none of which were deemed to be constructive or have any justification, nor were they detailed in the minutes! One can only wonder as to the exact nature of the suggestions and hope that they were simply mischievous!

TROPHY: Southend High School for Boys Junior Choir who won the Olive Owers Challenge Cup

*Fig 64: Prize Winners.*

Mrs. Pat Jacobson had landed the role of Chief Steward and set about detailing what the duties of the stewards should be, taking money at the door and selling programmes was not to be one of them. It was felt that the Treasurer should take charge of this aspect of the Festival as it fell under his responsibility. The profit from 1992 was not repeated in 1993, a deficit of £823 was reported, again this was covered by the interest from the Charity Commission account, but the aim, as always, was for the Festival to be self financing. Sun Life Assurance Company came to rescue with a sponsorship of

£1000 for two years. Matters were not helped by the venue charging an ex-gratia payment of £25 for the removal of furniture - particularly as all the furniture that needed to be moved from the church was moved by the stewards and the executive! To clear up any confusion the Venture Scouts were drafted in in 1994 to undertake the job, including the removal of the altar rails.

Entries were down a little in 1994 at just under 1,500 and another appeal for 'platform manners' was made. A reminder that 'skirts always look shorter on a platform' was given in the instructions to performers. Attention was also given to the archive with an appeal for missing programmes, syllabus' and articles to be found and donated if possible.

The 1995 Festival saw an increase in entries and a footnote in the minutes recalling that the minutes of 1911 had recorded the need for a large hall and no progress had been made! It was also of note that Sally Browne, as well as serving as the Vice Chairman, had now clocked up 10 years as Entries Secretary. Peggy Taffs was deserving of a special mention in 1995 for her skill with caligraphy. She had prepared 130 special certificates for the Festival in 1995. It was also reported that Rita Ellis, a long time supporter of the Festival had passed away, along with Winifred French who left a legacy of £500 to the Festival.

Entries for 1996 fell further to 1,324 and the choirs in particular did not enter in their usual numbers this year. However, there was a new category for orchestras and school big bands that captured the interest of local reporters with headlines of ' Tune up those violins, polish up the trumpets and clear the throat!' ending the Festival with a satisfactory declaration that 'the future of music is in safe hands with the children.' The final evening of Big Band classes was described as 'truly exciting'.

By 1997 Annette Forkin had joined the Executive Committee and embarked upon a project to computerise the administrative functions of the Festival. With her considerable computing expertise and the support of her late father, Ron Richardson, she designed a computer system for the Festival that went live in time for the 1997 Festival.  It is astounding to realise the amount of manual effort that went into preparing the attendance slips & criticism sheets in the past.  Sally Browne hand-wrote and double checked every competitor slip - over 1000 pieces of paper; Eileen Henderson-Williams was the Chief Recorder and also hand-wrote all the individual criticism sheets - again over 1000 pieces of paper! The computer system has continued to be used and enhanced every year, without doubt life is considerably easier in terms of planning the Festival due to her efforts. The Echo newspaper noted that ***'behind this huge and ambitious task lies almost a century of expertise in unleashing and judging an army of talent.'***

■ Sound byte – Annette Forkin has put the Festival on computer

***Fig 65:***
***Annette Forkin, Honorary Secretary.***

Dorothy Havis retired in 1997, handing the important role of official accompanist to Joanna Smith. It is clear that once caught up in the Festival it becomes a little like the Hotel California - you can never leave - and in 1997 long-serving members of the Festival were rewarded with a 25 year badge from the Federation.

*Fig 66: Dorothy & Joanna pictured in 1997.*

The familiar calls for an Arts Centre for the town were given a new source of hope in the form of Southend High School for Boys who were investigating the possibility of a Centre for the Performing Arts on the school premises. The Committee wrote in support of this although once again this plan did not come to fruition.

Harry Worsfold now became Treasurer to the Festival and remains in this post in 2011.

1998 saw the revisiting of the possibility of a keyboard class. The report for the 1998 Festival states that all five adjudicators were excellent and rather worryingly reports that 'thanks to scurrying stewards none of the string competitors were mislaid!'. Numbers were again down and it was felt that 'forces which disapprove strongly of competition' were to blame.

The position of official accompanist became vacant again in 1999 and initially it was decided that competitors should be requested to arrange their own accompaniment. However, there were strong objections to this and indeed it could become unmanagable to have large numbers of accompanists all waiting in turn to play for someone. Verina Wilson agreed to take on the role but only with support from other pianists. It is a hugely important role and one that can make or break a performance.

The end of this decade loomed and it finished on the amazing notes of Katie Ayers, 90 and Lillian Blunt, 79, winning the Parlour Songs class.

***Fig 67:* Katie Ayers & Lillian Blunt.**

By this time Katie Ayers had been associated with the Festival for many years. She moved to Leigh on Sea as a child and attended Westcliff High School for Girls. She was an accomplished pianist, taught by Vera Harding, and also played violin. Whilst her career was in banking, on retirement she devoted her energies to music. She could be found playing for keep fit classes, dance lessons and examinations, elderly people's clubs and choirs. She took a lively interest in the Festival and competed until a couple of years before her death.She donated two cups to the Festival one for Piano and one for Singing. These cups are still presented.

There were two other notable people who must be mentioned for their work with the Festival over many years.

Dorothy West BA, FTCL and Honor Jackson LRAM, both local music teachers. played a significant part in promoting the Festival and participating as Committee members.

Dorothy West was associated with the Festival as a competitor, Committee member, Convenor and Accompanist. She became an Executive Committee member in 1964 and when Madame Freda Parry stood down as Convenor of the Singing section in 1967, she became assistant to the new Convenor, Hilda Nevard. She became Singing Convenor herself in 1973. She was a great believer in the value of the Festival movement. She organised and attended every session of the Singing section and also accompanied many of the competitors who took part.

Honor Jackson had been Convenor of the Piano section since 1990 and she brought her knowledge, experience and wonderful organisational skills to bear in making this part of the Festival such a success.

A new century was about to begin, the Festival administration was in good shape, computerised, efficient, solvent and ready to face the 'noughties'.

## *The Doughty Deeds of Musical Valour Continue: 2000 - 2010.*

There is no doubt that the first decade of the new millennium has presented some exacting challenges for our world. Global warming, global terrorism, several wars and the collapse of global stock markets to name but a few. There have also been exciting discoveries to celebrate - the human genome and the oldest known planet - Methuselah at 12.7 billion years old. In the literary world there surely cannot be a child left who has not heard of Harry Potter, Carol Ann Duffy became the first woman Poet Laureate in its 341 year history and Harold Pinter was awarded the Nobel Prize for Literature. This decade also lost some of the most popular musicians and actors of the century in Sir John Guilgud, Peter Ustinov and Alex Guiness; Peggy Lee and Rosemary Clooney; George Harrison and Michael Jackson. Queen Elizabeth the Queen Mother and Princess Margaret also passed away.

The turn of the century also saw the passing of Peter Bayliss, the long standing Chairman of the Festival. He had undertaken practically every job and task required to keep the Festival going in over 60 years of involvement - commitment to a good cause clearly ran in his family, Uncle Horace had trained him well. It is appropriate in this the centenary year of the Festival to acknowledge the enormous contribution made by these men. Both men have cups awarded in their name each year. Sally Browne, who as Vice - Chairman had been standing in for Peter during the last months of his life, stepped up to the role and continues as both Entries Secretary and Chairman in 2011. Her involvement with the Festival spans some 33 years and her contribution cannot be overestimated. The year 2000 also saw the appointment of Annette Forkin as Honorary General Secretary - a position she still fills with the utmost skill. Pat Jacobson, Chief Steward since 1993, and Peggy Taffs, Chief Recorder who had been solely responsible for producing the beautifully scripted 'cup' certificates for many years, were both made Honorary Members, as was Eileen

Greaves, who had been General Secretary from 1981 - 1993. Pat Jacobson remains as a steward and stalwart supporter of the Festival today - she is also Harry Potter's (Daniel Radcliffe's) granny!

The Festival of 2000 was reported as going very well as usual, the minutes however indicate that there were one or two hiccups that had the team reaching for the smelling salts! One adjudicator gave 'some unexpected decisions' and another 'too readily accepted sub-standard playing from the seniors!'. The heating collapsed completely at the venue and there was a funeral on the 2nd day of the Festival for which we had of course to vacate the premises. If this wasn't enough to try the patience of the great and the good there was a shortage of stewards, and an off duty fire officer who had been in the audience the day before returned in his official capacity to advise on emergency signage and evacuation procedures. Finally, just to test the resolve of the Festival team the official accompanist withdrew at the last minute! The saving grace this year was perhaps that the newspaper coverage of the whole event was described as 'dismal' - as in non-existent!

Whilst behind the scenes may have been a little fraught this year the competitors were, as always, excellent. The Bobby Birn Memorial Prize for the highest mark in Strings was awarded to a young lad in the cello solo class. Christopher Gascoine scored 88 and 90 marks respectively in his classes to secure the prize. Speech and Drama classes contained a prepared prose class - when given a choice of several texts from which to choose a passage, 14 out of the 15 entrants chose a Harry Potter piece. The class was sponsored by Marcia Gresham - Marcia was a prolific winner of dance trophies in the Festivals of the 1970s and 80s - she is also Harry Potter's (Daniel Radcliffe's) Mum! Another famous name to emerge in this Festival is that of Hannah Tointon, Kara's sister, Hannah also currently enjoys a popular acting career in television. She was awarded the Olive Owers Plaque, achieving 89 marks for her recital of 'Uncle Fred' by Robert Fisher. In the Piano section

Benjamin Grosvenor, the future BBC Young Musician of the Year finalist, could also be heard at the age of 7 years playing 'Camp of the Gypsies' by F. Behr, gaining 90 marks and the L E Hyde Memorial Cup. The Thorn girls - Suzie, Tammy and Rebecca - took the woodwind and brass section by storm and Tiffany Redman and Alicia Toms were also highly successful in the singing classes. Lilian Blunt clinched the Katie Ayers Cup for parlour songs and Liz Elliott continued her success winning the Branchflower Family Challenge Cup and the Gilberts Challenge Cup.

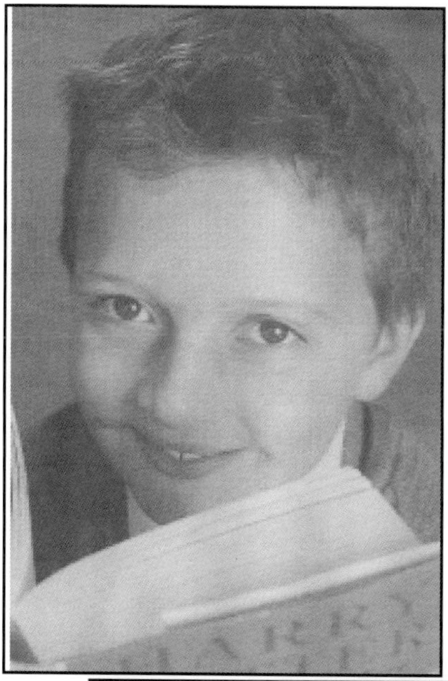

***Fig 68: Nicholas Cardosi with a signed copy of Harry Potter & the Philosopher's Stone.***

***Fig 69: Benjamin Grosvenor.***

*Fig 70: Tammy Thorn*

The focus in 2001 was to find another venue as costs had increased beyond the Festival's means. There had only been a small surplus of income to expenditure in 2000 and overall costs had increased by some £1000. It was at this time that Keymed agreed to sponsor the Festival and provided all of the stationery, this was a fantastic gesture and continued throughout the decade. Another boost to the coffers was the introduction of Gift Aid - this meant that the Festival could reclaim the tax on donations, again this has been - and continues to be - a great help to the financial viability of the whole enterprise.

A new venue at Crowstone Christian Centre was being considered and looked very promising for the Festival in 2002. The 2001 event took place at Highlands for the last time and it was of course the 90th anniversary of the Festival. It had its highs, lows and middling - muddling - situations. The press coverage was much better and the standards in woodwind were so high the adjudicator sent out for four boxes of chocolates so that he could award more prizes!

This was also the year of what is described in the minutes as the 'infamous geography trip!'. Either unknown or overlooked at the time of entry many competitors from one school were unable to compete as the schedule clashed with the trip. Full marks went to Liz Elliott and her rescheduling skills that accommodated most of the competitors at another time.

The Parry Bowl was now insured for some £4,500 and on permanent loan to the Council and a replacement trophy was awarded. The job of trophy maintenance was under new management and these were returned to the Festival in a highly polished state ready for the next batch of successful competitors. These included Benjamin Grosvenor again, this time for violoncello solo. He played Passepied - dall'Abaco and was awarded 94 marks. Benjamin also achieved three cups in piano and the Piano Pavilion Trophy for the highest marks overall. The winner of the solo own choice brass class, 10 - 11 years old, was Jordan Marshall with an interesting choice of 'The Wombling Song' by Mike Batt. Suzi Thorn also enjoyed continuing success gaining 96 marks in the concerto class. The fun continued with the first entry in the Festival of Luke Thornton, he entered the family class with his brother Ben, winning the Eileen Greaves Trophy for their very entertaining rendition of 'The Trail of the Lonesome Pine' (Harry Carroll). Luke continues to compete and particularly enjoys the comedy songs and songs from the shows.

Sandra Wilkes also entered the Festival for the first time, with daughter Elspeth as her accompanist and secured the Ivy Wright Challenge Trophy. Laura Burns sang her way to 4 trophies and the Premier Trophy overall.

***Fig 71:***
***Sandra & Elspeth Wilkes with Irene Jones***

Unfortunately two choirs withdrew at short notice leaving quite a gap in the schedule but the school choirs gave sterling performances with the Charles Waller Silver Shields i & ii going to St. Bernard's Chamber Choir, conducted by Hilary Pell, and West Leigh Boys Choirs respectively. The singing adjudicator was inspired to write to the Committee stating that the Festival had achieved 'a perfect balance of friendliness and formality that gave participants a sense of occasion but did not intimidate them.'

Whilst the 2001 Festival returned a surplus, funds were a cause of concern and it was decided that the subscriptions for friends of the Festival should be increased. There had not been an increase since 1992. A suggestion was put forward from the organisers of the Leigh Musical Festival that each should be held on alternate years as the local area was perhaps suffering from Festival overload. Whilst discussed by the Executive Committee the idea was eventually decided against.

Local teachers who enter their pupils into both competitions also felt that biennial festivals would be confusing.

The AGM of 2002 announced the deaths of three dedicated supporters of the Festival. Eileen Greaves, Ron Richardson and Joyce Birn. All tireless workers behind the scenes and supporters of music across the town.

As well as a new venue to get to grips with 2002 brought the new marking scheme from the Federation. Whilst it was fairly close to the one already in use there were some changes to consider, although the Committee elected to continue with marks, rather than move to a system of grades, which has proved to be a popular decision over time. The regular pre Festival meeting of the Executive Committee reported two new legacies had been received, one from the sisters of Doreen Bowyer and one from the estate of the late Ron Richardson. Both were to be invested and to be used to support annual prizes across four classes. Entries for 2002 were substantially lower than usual, despite the anticipated last minute rush that hasn't changed since 1911! With only 1088 entries a substantial deficit was anticipated. Two new 'helpers' joined the ranks, with Sue Greengrass and Sheila Kelleway taking up specific responsibilities for the Singing and Woodwind/Brass Sections respectively - a significant move towards setting up teams per Section. These ladies still work with the Festival - it seems that once bitten by the Festival bug you tend to stay for a long time!

The new venue of Crowstone Christian Centre proved highly successful, although there was not room for the piano classes there at the time and these were held at the Civic Centre. There was virtually no press coverage at all this year, but results were published on the internet for the first time. This was due to the generosity of ABC Music and the web management of WebWright's Brian Nichols. Publishing the results on the internet meant that it was no longer necessary to maintain three programmes on the Recorder's desk - one for the Festival records and two for the press.

The string section proved to be a little logistically

challenging with one group of eight cellists performing and winning first prize, the second prize went to a group of 6! Whilst the performing platform was accommodating, a minimum of 14 cellos in one space can clearly cause some congestion! There were also two other groups of young cellists competing in this class, although it isn't recorded how many cellos were in each.

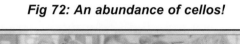

***Fig 72: An abundance of cellos!***

The Speech and Drama section saw an 'outstanding' performance from Gabrielle Stewart who recited 'Sarah' from The Little Princess and won both the Premier Bronze Medal class and the Ridley Batchelor Cup. The singing competition was of interest this year with mother and daughter competing against each other. Frances Hickling, the owner of a rather lovely soprano voice, entered the same class as her daughter Frankie. Frankie pipped Mum at the post with 1 mark. Frances however went on to win two further classes. Alicia Toms was also successful and went home with 3 trophies.

The Parlour Songs class was won by a gentleman named Walter Tee. Katie Ayers presented him with her cup - this was to be for the last time as Katie passed away early in 2003. Walter continues to compete.

Benjamin Grosvenor again enjoyed many successes at the Festival, with the piano Adjudicator commenting that 'here was an exceptional talent.' - very well foretold!

The post festival meeting saw some concerns raised about several issues. Prompting from teachers had been a little too intrusive, not to mention against the rules, and there had been some uninvited 'guests' in the public gallery of the Civic Centre. There had also been a national proposal that Churches should pay for music licenses if they held more than six concerts in any one year. This could potentially impact on the costs involved in holding the Festival in Church premises. It was also noted that the Festival had received another surprise guest with an impromtu visit from the Federation. The verdict was that Southend was a 'well-run and thriving' Festival. Well run festivals still need to be financially solvent and consideration had to be given to increasing entry fees and this was agreed. Another aspect to be introduced this year was the Criminal Records checks now required by law for those people working or volunteering in organisations that brought them into contact with children or vulnerable adults. The Federation were of great help in this matter and the local Council were extremely helpful in verifying paperwork required. The Executive Committee was required to produce its own Child Protection Policy and distribute it accordingly. This was created from scratch and took many hours of refining before it was acceptable - another job that fell to the Secretary. The Festival has always had a duty of care to junior performers but the law now required something far more substantial and although it was not yet compulsory for Festivals - not being classed as child care organisations - the Committee felt it wise to be pro-active and this was duly put in place.

Another substantial piece of work was the Federation's Moderation and Standardisation Drive. This was a major initiative for all Festivals as the Federation wanted to be classed as an educational body. There are several advantages to acquiring educational status in terms of copyright regulations and VAT. The idea was to be able to publish uniform marks / categories with associated descriptors and criteria for Federation Adjudicators to try and ensure consistency of marking year on year. This may sound familiar........!

A more immediate local initiative was to continue building

on the idea of making each section of the Festival independent and responsible for its own organisation to take some of the load off the Secretary. Again some things never change.....! One task that was brilliantly organised was that of the Chief Recorder duties: arranging for all the certificates to be written in advance, batched up and delivered to the Festival, and ensuring that all those working on the Recording desk were aware of how to prepare certificates for presentation and record the marks in the Official Programme - no light undertaking - and this was done by Doris Smith and Pat Porter - these ladies stepped down from the job only in 2010. This has always been a separate job, before Pat & Doris stepped in Eileen Henderson-Williams had completed the task for many years.

Councillor Howard Briggs, a past competitor, now became the Vice-President of the Festival and continues in this position in 2011 - another one captured!

It was decided to reinstate the Prize Winners' Concert in 2003 and this was sponsored in memory of Joyce Birn by her daughter, Pattie. It was a great success and a concert at the end of the Festival was to become a permanent feature once more. In the past it had been held several weeks after the Festival had ended and had caused some difficulties in retaining the interest of the public and the performers. It is currently held on the Sunday of the final weekend of the Festival and provides a lovely, celebratory end to two weeks of outstanding performance and triumph.

Entries were up for the 2003 Festival and most things went according to plan. There are some things that no amount of contingency planning can accommodate and the sight of the Adjudicator using the performers' instruments to demonstrate his points did not go down well with anyone - least of all the child who then had to play the instrument!

A strings session ended with time in hand and all the children played the set piece together led by the Adjudicator. Florian Cooper was the star of the strings this year with two cups and an honours certificate. The Blore family also created a lasting impression with all three boys enjoying various successes. One of our current highly versatile and successful competitors also made her first appearance at the Festival - Sophie Ann Chaplin delivered a respectable violin solo gaining second place in her class for under 9s. She was also successful in both piano and woodwind classes.

In the speech and drama Special Needs class the group performance produced a tie between the dd'Arts and Kingsdown School - two gold medals were awarded. There was only one soul brave enough to enter the spontaneous improvisation class where the competitor had to create a scene around an object given to them on the spot by the Adjudicator. Simone Stewart was quick enough and gained honours marks of 85, she also won the Shakespeare class and the Margaret Stone Memorial Bowl.

Don Collard made a welcome return to the Festival at the age of 80. He had not competed for fifty years and was delighted to win the Katie Ayers Cup in the Parlour Songs class. This was the beginning of several years of good friendship and rivalry between Don and Walter Tee - two of our older gentlemen competitors.

***Fig 73: Don Collard.***

Don and Louise Collard had been strong supporters of music in the town for many years. Louise had also been the

Mayoress. Another couple who had supported the Festival were Frank & Muriel Muddiman. Frank contacted the Festival wishing to donate a trophy in memory of his wife, Muriel. In keeping with our recently introduced practice he produced a beautiful written tribute to her, which is presented with the trophy to the winner each year. Sadly, Frank passed away shortly before the first presentation of the trophy, but it was presented by their son, Colin and their two daughters Margaret and Jill. They travel to the Festival each year to present the trophy.. Wherever possible sponsors of classes - or their relatives - are asked if they wish to attend the class and present the winner with the prize. Many people do come to do this and are delighted to know that their donation is being cherished both by those who win and by the Festival.

As with some competitors, sometimes an Adjudicator stands out for particular praise, in 2003 Kenneth Bowen was labelled as 'one of the old school, he did not impose his personality on the event but concentrated wholly on the performers'.

For 2004 the usual business of the Festival Committee was undertaken, classes were added, prizes changed - in this case Gold Medals were to be awarded with the trophies for all age groups. Whilst this had a cost implication it was felt that when the trophy had to be handed back it would be good for the performer to have something to keep. The cost implication was covered by Peter Parsons. Peter continues to cover the cost of the medals and is an extremely generous benefactor of the Festival, he also gives freely of his time as a steward.

In terms of cost implications it was time to get tough with those friends who had not paid their subscriptions for the year and in some cases two years. One not only paid up the arrears but paid for the following year as well! Entries were up by 126 for the 2004 Festival and as usual the vast majority of them arrived at Sally's post box in the last week.

Some familiar names were back, Sophie Ann continued to improve her string playing, her piano, woodwind and her singing. Dee Hunter, who was on her second year of competing did very well in the piano classes winning two cups and continued to compete for several more years. She has gone on to follow a professional career as a pianist and singer.

***Fig 74: Dee Hunter at the Festival 2006.***

The event that stood out in the 2004 Festival was that of the Adjudication in the singing section. Marilyn Hill-Smith is a highly experienced Adjudicator and is known for not taking any prisoners, and on several occasions declined to award trophies for performances that she felt did not merit them. One such performance was that given by Don Collard, whilst disappointed, Don - ever the gentleman - is quoted as saying:

***'She is charming, highly gifted and a very tough cookie - but very fair. .... if you are foolish enough to put your head on the block you stand the chance of it being chopped off!'***

Laura Burns did come up to the Adjudicator's standards and secured four cups! Overall it was a year of low marking in the singing section and some people were unhappy about the decisions made, but Marilyn Hill-Smith was not a lady to compromise - she looks for intonation, accuracy and presentation and if she can't find it she will say so. One competitor sang 'an over ambitious song and did not make a good job of it' - she was reported as trying to be constructive and urged the competitor 'not to get bad advice from her teacher or mother that would lead her to spoil her voice.'

On the other side of the marking coin was the Adjudicator for strings who gave exceptionally high marks to everyone!

This is what makes the case for the standardisation of marking - there needs to be some level of consistency across the board so that teachers can judge what classes their pupils are ready for, and pupils can be confident that they are able to reach a standard and perform well. When going through the syllabus and selecting a suitable class for a pupil it is important to match the standard required with the standard reached. It is also important to make sure that the right child is entered for the right class with the right information on what they will be expected to perform.

There were one or two teething problems at the new venue. In particular a mother and baby class had not received notification that their meeting was cancelled due to the Festival. They duly arrived with tiny babies to take over a practice room. The noise was somewhat distracting and despite being informed of the cancellation of their meeting for the following week they still turned up!

Noise from the other rooms and facilities at the centre is a particular problem and we now have a solution that everyone involved tries to avoid doing - the noise reducing curtains! These heavy velvet curtains are hung across the door each year and whoever draws the short straw puts them up!

Still in search of ways to make the Secretary's life bearable there was debate over whether to leave the Newsreader class behind this year. It ran from 2000 - 2005 with an annual prize from BBC Essex of a trip around the station at Chelmsford and an interview. They would send one of their newsreaders along each year to help adjudicate the class. Whilst it had been popular, the Secretary had to come up with the ideas and write the scripts for it.

The 2005 Festival saw another increase in entries with 1388 (11 in the Newsreader class!) and another new venue for the first weekend, as the Crowstone Christian Centre was not available. The two days of competition were held in Alleyn Court School and it turned out to be a delightful venue.

***Fig 75:***
***Mark Thornton & Shoshana Burns, winners of the Newsreader Class, with BBC Essex presenter Roger Buxton.***

The noise reducing curtains also helped to stifle some of background noise at the Crowstone Christian Centre.

The Festival of 2005 was overshadowed somewhat by an unprecedented amount of illness and injury amongst the stewards, things went smoothly with the Secretary working ridiculous hours to ensure everything was covered and those still standing, working 10 - 12 hour days every day. A crisis had been reached and more stewards were needed.

This year's supply of medals also proved to be problematic - they arrived with a sticky substance coating them and Harry Worsfold, the Treasurer, took them all home and washed them with only a slight improvement!

The Festival welcomed two new Official Accompanists in Marjorie Sale and Paul McDowell who both did an excellent job. There was a union of two talented families this year, the Blores teamed up with the Walters and formed a cello quintet. They were successful in both the HSBC String Group Trophy class and won the Chamber Music prize.

It was with great sadness that the deaths of Honor Jackson, the Convenor of the Piano Section, and Dorothy West, Official Accompanist and Convenor of the Singing Section, were reported. A former pupil of Honor stated 'I feel her presence and personality in all the music I play' and Dorothy is remembered as 'a great believer in the Festival movement, always ready with a smile, sadly missed.'

Another supporter of the Festival, Mrs. Tunnicliffe, also died in 2005. As founder and Headmistress of a local private school, St. Hilda's, her pupils had entered the Festival for many years with some success.

A special executive meeting was held in early 2006 to discuss the future of the Festival. Volunteering in a good cause is one thing, having that cause take over your life is quite another, and something had to be done to ensure that the running of the Festival did not fall to one small band of people. We needed a recruitment drive! We needed a work plan!

Music Festival success for St Hilda's

***Fig 76: St. Hilda's pupils.***

Sally continued as Chairman and Entries Secretary, Annette continued as Honorary General Secretary, Harry took a break from being Treasurer and Mark Brudenell stepped into the role. Elizabeth Elliott became Convenor of the Singing Section and Louise Manders agreed to become the Speech & Drama Convenor, Margaret Rowan (supported by Section Secretary Eileen Greaves) became Convenor of the Piano Section and Strings got the benefit of Jena Pang and Emma Peake, and Woodwind and Brass continued unchanged. Whilst the General Secretary would pull everything together, the nitty gritty of each section needed to be dealt with on an individual section basis and each section had to be staffed. Whilst the key people in each team are the Section Secretary and the Convenor, each selection panel consists of several local teachers who use their experience and skill to choose appropriate pieces in music and drama for competitors to perform. It is a difficult task and takes time and research to get right.

The pre Festival meeting for 2006 reported that entries were stable, although there were more from adults this year and less from children. It was thought there would now be a clash with the 11+ examinations, as these had been moved from February to November. Louise Manders had embarked on a serious sponsorship drive and secured several new sponsors for classes, greatly aiding the budget.

At this time Sue Greengrass became interested in sorting out the Festival Archives and Trophy Catalogue. The job was undertaken by Sue and her daughter Alex, and they produced the first detailed inventory of the cups and trophies awarded since the start of the Festival in 1911. Harry had also done a sterling job of finding information buried in the last 95 years worth of minutes. This archive has provided a fascinating insight into the history of the Festival.

Crowstone Christian Centre again proved to be a very good venue and with a new centre manager, Emer McNeela, the competitions went smoothly. There was some confusion in the Chamber Music class as a saxophone quartet played a startling and unexpected rendition of 'Has Anybody Seen My Gal?!'. This was the only class available to this group due to the age of the

competitors - the age groups were refined for the following year! The Junior Recital class was reported as outstandingly good and the Blores & Walters families again teamed up to achieve success with the HSBC Bank String Group Trophy.
Luke Thornton also continued to improve and refine his performances.

A departure from the usual business of the Festival came in 2007 when it was decided to host the Freda Parry Scholarship Competition. This scholarship provides a substantial monetary prize to young singers who are pursuing a professional career. At first it was thought that the Festival would not be able to host the competition at all but with the co-operation of two local choirs, who used the venue for practice on two sessions during the Festival, and agreed to change their arrangements, it was possible to include 'The Parry' in the Festival programme. This provided an afternoon of outstanding entertainment as young singers performed their recitals. The winner in 2007 was Alex Kidgell.

An armful of trophies for singer Luke

***Fig 77:* Luke Thornton.**

In 2007 Sally was awarded the long service badge - perhaps it should be renamed as long-suffering badge especially when it comes to sorting out the post. The usual last rush of entries was actually broken down in this year to show that the week before the closing date Sally had received 102 entries, on the Thursday before the closing date this number had risen to 680 and the following two days saw a further 620 letters drop through her post box. Songs from the Shows for 12 - 15 years old accounted for 57 of these. It seems that this age group in particular like to sing the more popular songs and the class was divided into 3 sub classes to accommodate them all. Strings however had 291 entries the highest for this section in 9 years. It was clear some new music stands would be needed and five were purchased.

Following the death of Honor Jackson a new trophy was to be awarded in her name - The Honor Jackson Memorial Trophy for Piano Playing. This was first presented in 2006 to James Choi by Honor's husband, Bill. The Dorothy West Memorial Prize was won by Laura Burns.

A new young voice also appeared in the singing section - April Goss, she won the Frith Family Cup for 9 - 12 year olds and continues to compete. Walter Tee had donated a cup for the Sing & Play class, this was won by Jonathan Morell, another promising young musician. Luke Thornton was not put off by the fact that he was the only boy, if not in the world then certainly in the Songs from the Shows class, as there were 20 girls. He won the class with 89 marks.

Following the 2007 Festival Denise Raynsford resigned her position as Vice Chairman. She had given many years of service to the Festival, firstly as a 'dancing Mum' with Pat Jacobson, ensuring the dance classes went well, helping behind the scenes and of course supporting their daughters, Joanna Allnatt and Marcia Gresham. She had taken on the role of Secretary and then Vice Chairman and now wished to step back a little - only a little as she still helps with the Festival, as does Pat, and both are Honorary Friends. Sheila Kelleway now became the Vice Chairman.

All Adjudicators at the 2007 Festival sent their congratulations on a very enjoyable and successful Festival. One in particular, Kate Elmitt, had gone out of her way to put the younger competitors at their ease, wearing 'quaver' earrings - whether this was a model of the actual note or a popular crispy snack is not made clear! Although one Adjudicator is reported as having a dry sense of humour 'not appreciated by all!'.

Unfortunately the 2007 Festival ended with a financial deficit. Adjudication fees and expenses had increased and there was nothing for it but to increase the fees charged. It seems to work in 4 year cycles, the last increase had been in 2003. The season ticket for the whole Festival was to be increased from £3 to £8 and subscriptions from friends were to increase from £6 to £8 with £10 for a couple.

It was again decided to host the competition for the Parry scholarship within the programming of the Festival. It was hoped to attract more competitors and the competition was opened to the whole of Essex.

The Festival received an astonishing legacy this year. £25,000 was given from the estate of William Bishop. This very generous and welcome injection into the Festival finances is securely invested. Although 2011 interest rates leave a great deal to be desired, the capital does go a long way to providing some financial security for the future of the Festival.

The Festival has collected a large number of trophies and cups over the years and despite several other Festivals disposing of their old trophies and cups, Southend Executive Committee has always voted to keep ours. Along with the archives of Festival programmes and Syllabus and newspaper reports, there was quite an accumulation of 'stuff'. The vast majority of this 'stuff' was stored in Annette's loft and Harry's kitchen, alongside all the equipment required to stage the Festival. A storage place was needed. This was eventually found in the basement of the Crowstone Christian Centre.

The Festival of 2008 was a break even year. The Strings

section Adjudicator was especially helpful in terms of his expenses claims - he ran to and from the venue as part of his training for the London Marathon! Another was partial to giving impromptu demonstrations on the French Horn - having brought his own with him for the purpose - and a young boy named Ewan Dunlop will probably not forget playing 'When the Saints' with him. Another unforgettable moment was provided by Walter Tee and his rendition of 'Miss Hooligan's Christmas Cake'. He won the Thornton Trophy for most entertaining performance in the singing section.

The most cellos in one place record was broken this year with the HSBC trophy going to a group of 9 of them!

***Fig 78: Walter Tee, 2011.***

In 2009 thoughts turned to the plans for the centenary celebrations. Although the cash flow was once again tight, the financial difficulties around the world were refected in everyone's budget. Interest rates had declined to a rather drastic level and although the capital balance remained healthy, it was clear that some reserves would need to be utilised. A sub-committee was set up to explore how and when to celebrate the fantastic achievement of the 100th year of the Festival.

Entries were down as expected, although seven children's choirs had entered, giving a total of 260 children to deal with on choir morning. Choir morning is a miracle of order out of abject chaos! The stewarding is of vital importance and it has to be organised with military precision. This amazing feat is smoothly and seamlessly achieved by the forward planning of

Sue Greengrass and Liz Elliott. The stewards are all allocated jobs, rooms are allocated to each choir, each room clearly labelled and teachers and children are herded around the venue with absolute precision! Upstairs to the gallery, downstairs to the side of the room, up front on the floor - everything and everyone in their right place - we hope! When one choir session has finished a quick change of room labels ensures the Festival is ready for the next group. The parents are somewhat more difficult to organise. There are only two places they can be - in the audience or at the refreshment area. Even the infamous noise reducing curtains cannot keep out the loud rumble of conversation as one set wait for their children's school to take to the stage. Nevertheless, it is a joyful morning and much anticipated by the schools, the choirs, the parents and all of the Festival team. All that remains is to provide a dark room to lie down in when it's over!

Sadly 2009 saw the passing of Don Collard, just before the Festival started. He had continued to compete after his comeback at the age of 80, and was always a worthy competitor. The Festival went off very smoothly once more. There were the usual strange events such as Class 267, whilst clearly stated to be a 'duet for any orchestral instrument and piano' confusion reigned when two flute players took to the stage! One Adjudicator was described as rather 'stingy' when it came to giving out the medals and another as 'the best adjudicator for some time'. The Adjudicators are booked at least one year in advance and all come highly recommended, but different folks do have different strokes! The Federation has a list of recommended adjudicators who are trained and mark to an agreed system, and therefore the Festival will use Federation Adjudicators as much as possible to try and ensure consistency in the marking from section to section and year to year.

The newspapers reported the 2009 Festival as a 'showcase for excellence' at 98 years old.

The piano section was still being held at the Civic Centre and it was decided to bring the whole Festival under one roof for

2010. The Civic Centre terms and conditions for hire were to change quite dramatically and it would no longer be suitable for the needs of the Festival. Let the logistical nightmare begin! By running sections simultaneously, dovetailing three hour sessions it was hoped that all the classes would fit in - and they did.

Clara Roberts stood down from her two choirs in 2010 and the Claire Singers donated a new award to mark her exceptional dedication to choir music. This handsome cut glass rose bowl is awarded to the choir that gives the most moving performance.

***Fig 79: Angie Wicks***

***Fig 80: Colin Wyatt***

***Fig 81: West Leigh Junior School***

The 2010 Festival plans started with a surplus of £400 - a welcome surprise, but reserves would need to be used. The plans for the centenary celebrations started to take shape with a floral display on the cliffs arranged, an exhibition of the Festival Archives at Southend library, a formal dinner dance, a special centenary programme and a book. Another small army - well regiment - of volunteers got down to work. Special classes were to be arranged - some of them including the pieces that were used in 1911. In the meantime November 2010 would soon arrive and all the usual - and some new - arrangements had to be put into place. Arrangements were made for the piano to delivered to the Crowstone Christian Centre and for it to be tuned throughout the Festival. This did not allow for the problem of a squeaky pedal which was very off putting, especially for young competitors. The emergency contingency plan saw Annette once again on hands and knees wedging something under the pedal until the fault could be rectified!

Choir morning was the usual apparent order out of chaos. An idea to keep waiting parents and their cups of tea away from the immediate vicinity of the hall and let them wait at the reception area went well - until the next set of parents and children arrived. As soon as one group were moved back to the refreshment area they were sent back out to the reception! The solution was to call the next class and ask the children to line up outside the door and be very quiet. The effect on the parents was marvellous! All remained relatively quiet! That is until the door steward clapped enthusiastically at the end of a performance, forgetting that the ribbon to keep the door shut was firmly around her wrist! The resulting slams of the door with each clap reverberated around the building!

Performing at the Festival can be quite a trial for the competitors, it can also change the most level headed Mum into a nervous wreck. As the time for a morning class approached a clearly harassed Mum arrived in reception with a small boy, clutching the pink entry slip. His name could not be found on the list, on further questioning Mum took a horrified look at her son and yelped 'Wrong child!' before hurrying off to collect the correct son from school!

As the Festival has grown older so have the people associated with it. Dorothy Havis, the Official Accompanist to the Festival for many years passed away just before the Festival commenced in 2010. Once again here was someone who left a lasting legacy of musical expertise behind her.

As the plans come together for the centenary Festival amongst the excitement and pride there is also time to reflect and remember everyone in the past who worked so hard to make the Festival what it is today. It is also a time to give heartfelt thanks to those who carry the responsibility for it today.

Gladys Mude, when asked about her experiences in the Festival said with a chuckle that it was her poor Father who suffered from it the most;

> ***'Every November he would say to me***
> ***"That's it then, Gladys, there will be no tea cooked in this house for a fortnight! Your Mother is off to the Festival."***
> ***I decided I had better join her or starve! He couldn't cook you see.'***

So perhaps it is fitting to thank all those husbands, wives, kids and families who support the Festival team, and we hope will continue to do so for another century.

***PS: Just in case anyone is wondering whether I had forgotten - the pier caught fire in 2005!***

***Fig 82: The Claire Singers Bowl***

## *Festival Memories are made of this .......*

***Sally Browne, Chairman, Southend Musical Festival.***

Having been 'volunteered' to help record marks in 1978 (and not missing a Festival since) I little thought that I would be Chairman in the Centenary year of 2011. So much has happened in the thirty-three years that I have been involved with the Festival. Eileen Greaves was the secretary then and did nearly everything on the organising side herself with just the typing of the syllabus and programme being done by Dorothy Havis on a heavy manual typewriter. All competitor slips were written by hand as were the crit-sheets and the numbers entering were as high then as now. All certificates were printed 1st, 2nd, 3rd , honours etc so all names had to be written in at the end of a class when the marks were awarded - quite difficult when there were over twenty in a class and you were the only one on duty!

I have also been Entries Secretary since 1984. When I started helping, John Curtis who was Treasurer and Peter Bayliss who was then Vice Chairman had the entries sent to them and they were 'filed' unopened in a box and tipped in one huge pile on John's dining room table, we then spent two days opening and sorting them into classes before we could process them in any way and they could then go to the Secretary for timing and typing. Things have come a long way since then and computers have helped to stream-line the whole system.

During my thirty-three years various venues have been used, Civic Centre in what is now the café, one of the Committee rooms and the Council Chamber, Clifftown Church Hall, Trinity Argyll Church, St Saviour's Kings Road, Alleyn Court School, Leigh Community Centre, Blenheim Music Centre as well as Highlands Methodist Church and now Crowstone Christian Centre. It has been truly a 'Southend' Festival !!

***Annette Forkin, Honorary General Secretary, Southend Musical Festival.***

As a keen competitor in recorder-playing and school choir classes at the Southend Musical Festival during the 1960's, little did I think that I would eventually become Honorary General Secretary of the Association! I have many fond memories of my endeavours during those early years - some very successful, other less so, but all of them great fun.

My career then took me in other directions, and I spent 25 years designing computer systems for large City banks and financial institutions - music was still an important part of my life, but working long hours, commuting, and travelling within Europe and the Far East meant that I had to be content with listening, rather than playing. In 1997, however, I had reached a point where I was able to fulfil a long-standing ambition to retire from the world of IT before I completely lost my enthusiasm for it, in order to devote time and energy to other interests. By happy coincidence - and an introduction carefully engineered by my late father, Ron Richardson - I was able to re-enter the Festival movement and use the IT and organisational skills I had developed during my career to assist it via computerisation. I also rejoined the Southend Chamber Music Club after many years' absence, and started playing again. Now, playing - and teaching - the recorder has become a major part of my life and I have the influence of the Music Festival to thank for it.

In the year 2000, following the death of our most valued and respected Chairman, Peter Bayliss, Sally Browne (who had been standing in for Peter during the last months of his illness) became Chairman in her own right, and Denise Raynsford (a tireless and hard-working Secretary for seven years) became Vice-Chairman, leaving me to take over as Secretary. This has been a very difficult, but tremendously rewarding task, made possible only by the dedication and hard work of our wonderful Committee and Stewards and the support of our Members, Friends and Sponsors.

I have been privileged to serve an Association for which I

have great admiration and respect, and hope that my contribution has helped it to keep pace with changing tastes and approaches to music and drama, whilst remaining true to the Objects of the Festival established in 1911. I have never forgotten the nervous anticipation that always preceded an appearance at the Music Festival, and the inevitable "butterflies" that would plague me immediately prior to going on stage. The ability to conquer these feelings, and produce a successful and effective performance is something that has stood me in very good stead throughout my career and beyond - it is my fervent hope that the Southend Musical Festival will continue to provide this invaluable support and encouragement to performers for many, many years to come.

**My first Festival as Secretary**

The first day of my first Festival as Secretary provides a perfect illustration of "the best laid schemes of mice and men oft go awry"! True to form, I had planned, planned and planned again for what I thought would be every possible eventuality - but I had NOT planned for the heating system at Highlands Methodist Church to break down on the morning of the first day, resulting in the emergency installation of two enormous "space heaters" (like floor-standing jet engines), powered by 4-foot high cylinders tastefully arranged at the rear of the seating area! Following the vicar's hurried 5-minute instruction course on how to operate these monsters, I was on my own. After a quick blast of heat, we realised that they were far too noisy to use during classes, so we switched them off. This resulted in the Strings adjudicator donning coat, scarf, gloves and resigned expression throughout the morning as the miserable November weather seeped into the building and chilled us all to the bone. Until the Mobile Library arrived, that is! No-one had told me that it would need to use the car-park that day, and I therefore had to stop the proceedings while people went and moved their cars - which seemed like an ideal opportunity to provide a quick blast from the space heaters. As nothing else was happening, a sea of faces turned to watch as, with scribbled instructions in hand, I turned on the tap of the gas cylinder and confidently straddled the space heater in order to operate the supply button low down on one side, followed by the ignition on the other. There are many vivid recollections of this moment which have been recounted over the years, and usually involve visions of me taking off through the roof of the church and disappearing into the stratosphere - but only I know the true horror of releasing quantities of gas into the church whilst failing to ignite it! I tried - and failed - many times. Too many, in fact, because the church was now so full of gas that - with perfect irony - we had to open the windows. Ah ... happy memories!

***Elspeth Wilkes, Professional Musician.***

I have very fond memories of performing at the Southend music festival from the age of 7 to the age of 18 and beyond! When my teacher first suggested entering, I was nervous about the whole aspect of 'competition' which was something very different from the discipline of taking piano exams. I soon realised, however, that this aspect of competition and the opportunity to perform to an enthusiastic and supportive audience, not to mention the constructive feedback from a professional musician, was invaluable and so enjoyable. It wasn't long before I was entering every class in my age bracket that I was eligible for, from Bach to 20th Century. I used to count down the days to the festival beginning from the moment I received the slips with my dates and times on and would eagerly await the publication of the programme so I could see how many people I was up against and what they were playing!

As soon as the festival was over, I always experienced a little period of sadness that it was all finished for another year!

I feel that I was very fortunate to have performed for so many years at the festival and that the experiences, and the people involved with the festival, gave me a huge amount of help and encouragement for my future musical career. I still work as a pianist, accompanist, repetiteur and musical director in London and the South East and feel that I owe a lot of my success and continuing enjoyment of my musical career to the way in which the festival contributed greatly to my formative years.

***Gladys Mude, MBE, Former competitor 1930s - 1960s. Choir Mistress, Selection Panel member piano and singing.***

My mother was very involved in the Festival and it was natural that I would compete and, later on in life, become part of the Festival team. I have lovely memories of competing and enjoying some success, even winning cups and trophies occasionally. I remember being about 17 years old and having a crush on one of the Adjudicators - he was such a lovely, kind man - I can't remember if I won that year or not, but it didn't matter!. I had a soprano voice and took part in the recital classes but I did enjoy the British Folk Song classes. I moved away from Southend as a young woman to train as a teacher, but even then I would visit in November and compete at the Festival. On my return to Southend I became a volunteer at the hospital and arranged the nurses choir.

I continued to sing myself and was a member of the Freda Parry Choir that won the competition at the Festival of Britain in 1951.

It was wonderful to be invited to the Festival in 2010 to present the Mude Challenge Cup to the winner. This cup was actually donated by my mother and it is lovely to know that it is still be awarded. Music has been a very important part of my life and looking back I have enjoyed every part of it.

*Sadly Gladys passed away in June 2011 prior to the publication of this book.*

***Luke Thornton - Competitor.***

My first experience at the Southend Musical Festival was at the age of seven. My older brother Ben and I entered the Family Class and sang 'The Trail of the Lonesome Pine' and gained First Place. This was a big confidence booster for me and I have been taking singing lessons regularly since then with Janice Baker and have entered the Southend Festival annually for the last 10 years.

I have been fortunate to have gained many trophies and medals over these years gaining over 90 marks several times and my highest mark was 91 with "Rocking in Rhythm". I have always listened to the adjudicators' remarks and always tried to act upon their constructive criticism. I have learned to "find it amusing" when adjudicators contradict each other rather than get upset about it. "It's just one person's opinion" is my approach and I'm just happy to be given the platform to perform for my family.

I have sung in all the different singing classes - from Unaccompanied Folk Songs to Modern Ballads but I enjoy the Musical Show Songs the best.

I would like to thank all the committee and volunteers at the Festival for all their time and effort that has enabled me to perform and learn so much over the years. I am currently training in Performing Arts at college and hope to continue with my singing.

***Harry Worsfold, Honorary Treasurer.***

I was invited to become Treasurer of Southend Musical Festival in 1997 when my friend, Roger Calton, who is now the Independent Financial Adviser for the Festival, was working at the Citizen's Advice Bureau, Southend. At the time Peter Bayliss, the Chairman of the Festival, was also working there and he asked Roger if he knew anyone who would be willing to take on the Treasurer role - Roger volunteered me.

I attended the Annual General Meeting and was duly elected. Little did I realise that I would become involved in far more than just keeping the books! Over the years I have become an assistant to Annette, the Secretary and we have developed a great friendship and partnership. Her expertise in IT has helped me enormously over recent times when she has coached me in the use of the laptop which is proving to be a great benefit in my work.

The accounts have expanded over the years as the Festival has grown in popularity and we rely very much on our bank interest income on capital to offset the ever increasing costs of running the Festival.

The annual Festival is my busiest time, collecting all the takings daily, summarising, banking and then analysing the results for comparison with the previous year. There have been many anecdotal and highly amusing incidents over the years but everyone pulls together.

The centenary year should be a particularly enjoyable one, with special classes, lots of cash prizes and much to celebrate.

***Gerald Usher, Executive Committee Member, Federation Representative, Choirmaster, Teacher.***

As a teenage pianist I played popular and dance music fluently but wasn't much good at the classics - so the local Festival seemed a closed book to me. When I became Head of Music at Rayleigh it was an established tradition for groups from the school to compete each year, so I decided to put my choirs, bands and orchestras to the test and we did quite well.

Competition was often formidable but my secondary modern 11 - 16 year olds met the challenge magnificently and achieved notable results. From 1967 we became Fitzwimarc Comprehensive and upped our game to win most of the classes we entered in the ensuing years.

How did we do it? Perhaps the most important factor was to focus on general musicianship. The empathy in which we all worked and the sheer fun we got out of it still evoke fond memories and many long-lasting friendships were forged through Festival participation. It was all about working together - in harmony!

***Joanne Burch, Competitor 1990s, Dance teacher.***

Thinking back to my school years and competing in the music festival brings a big, wide smile to my face. The competition was fun but also very nerve wracking for us students. I always remember having butterflies in the pit of my stomach when arriving. Most of my friends would compete as well so it was always lovely and comforting to see them, even though they were just as nervous as I was.

I remember clearly sitting in the hall listening to other pupils recite their poems or acting pieces, desperately trying to check out the competition but going through my own lines at the same time. The Adjudicators were always very friendly and reassuring. I had a terrible cough through one competition and the Adjudicator was so nice she gave me a glass of water and told me to carry on when I was ready - I still took first prize. It was a special day and I will always remember it.

Taking part in the Festival gave me great confidence in later life to be able to speak to others, strangers and crowds alike. The Festival is a fantastic grounding for young pupils who enjoy verse speaking, acting and singing, it encourages you to continue with it into later life. I am now 26 years old and still very much enjoy all that is musical. The memories of the Festival will always stay with me as it was a special time in my life

**Sandra Gundy, Music & Drama teacher, Past HLR Royal Academy for the Associated Board.**

I first competed at the Festival as a child in 1950. It was a very large class and we all sang 'The Fairy Song'. I remember being recalled to sing again as the Adjudicator could not make up his mind, not good for the nerves!

My family and friends were always singing, it was a huge part of our lives, at one stage my sister Stephanie and I belonged to seven choirs! We were very fortunate to be encouraged and supported by our parents and teachers, especially Madame Freda Parry, who was quite inspirational in her approach to music. Horace Bayliss was always a very comforting presence at the Festival, he would stand at the side of the platform at Clifftown reassuring us as it was our turn to perform.

I clearly remember the wonderful choral competitions, there was always great difficulty getting us onto the stage, the choirs were so large. The atmosphere would buzz particularly on the last night for the Gold Medal and Oratorio classes. You would find people standing three deep around the edge of the hall - it wouldn't be allowed today, but it led to a fabulous atmosphere. The standards were so high and you really couldn't begin to guess who might win, it was exciting to be there and be a part of it.

There were three ladies who were always there, in the same seats for every class of the Festival, they never missed a session. Mrs. Bayliss - (Horaces' wife), Mrs. Crowe - (a miniscule lady), and Mrs. Mude - (Gladys' Mother) they were season ticket holders, they were also famous as knitters! Many Adjudicators would look around to identify the clickety clack of the needles!

I entered both singing, choral and Drama classes and won the Shakespeare Cup along with others. I continued competing with the Freda Parry Choir and eventually became the conductor. The Parry Singers continued to enjoy a great deal of success and disbanded while still winning. Following her death a Trust fund was established to provide a bursary for young student singers and I am now Chairman of that Trust.

As a music and drama teacher I entered my own pupils into the Festival over the years and another connection with it was through the Ridley Studios and Peggy Batchelor. The Ridley Studios was a thriving school from the mid 1950s and continues today. It was so vibrant and taught right across the arts. The Festival provided a great stepping stone and arena for performance before examinations, giving pupils the opportunity to be tested in front of an audience and the Adjudicator.

Despite the shaky knees and nerves I have very fond memories of the Festival, both as a teacher and serving on the selection committee and of course as a competitor and the lovely feelings of relief when it was over!

**Louise Manders, Speech & Drama Convenor, Teacher.**

Ever since I was very young, I can vividly remember spending many happy hours at the festival both as a competitor and as a member of the audience. My parents, Mick and Beryl Scholfield (both Mayors of Southend in their own right, with my mother later becoming a Freeman of the Borough) were life-long supporters. They encouraged all four of us to appreciate the value and immeasurable benefits of being a part of this celebrated annual event. My mother's memory lives on in the Recital Classes and how proud she would have been to have known that her love of performance continues to be remembered.

On a personal note, over the years I have watched with pride so many students enthusiastically rehearse their pieces, whether individually or within a group. As each pupil went on to perform in front of an audience, the advantages of taking part in such an event became abundantly clear. It has not only been a stepping stone for many young people to choose theatre and music-based subjects as a career path – with performing arts establishments both near and far, using the competitors as an essential talent source - but it has also been a vital element of self-improvement for each child to develop social and performance skills that will prove invaluable throughout their adult lives.

Southend Musical Festival has given and will continue to give each and every willing entrant – irrespective of age or ability – the opportunity to build confidence and shine.

**Anne Jones, Secretary Singing Section.**

I think I am one of the odd ones out on the committee, as I am non-musical in that I don't teach music, play an instrument or sing! My introduction to the festival started when my very musical friend Liz asked me if I fancied being a steward during the 2010 festival. I attended some sessions (mostly children's classes), which were very enjoyable. Having sat in the audience of many similar events over the years watching my own children and worrying about the outcome, it was rather nice to be able to enjoy the performances and be impartial!

Shortly after the festival Liz asked me if I would like to take over the position of Secretary to the Singing Section for 2012 when the current secretary Sue bows out after many years. So here I am, getting to grips with who's who, watching how Sue keeps it all running smoothly, and hoping I can do the same next year!"

***Walter Tee, Competitor.***

I have been competing in music festivals since 1997. I came to Southend Festival in 1998 for the first time and I have competed 10 times since then. As a child I was a church chorister but grew up and got on with life without much further interest in singing. On my retirement I was visiting a friend and came across a syllabus for the Stratford Festival and decided to have a go. I took singing lessons, including Lieder for which I had to learn German! I also belonged to a music hall group which gave good training for festivals as you had to learn all the songs by heart.

The Southend Festival is like an extension of my family, everyone is always so welcoming. I have sung with most of the Official Accompanists - Dorothy West, Joanna Smith and Paul McDowell and I always rehearse. I enjoyed a lovely friendly rivalry with the late Don Collard and like Don suffered at the hands of Marilyn Hill-Smith. I remember her as being quite ruthless, she felt that my timing was too slow and told me the audience would have to go home before I'd finished!!

I really enjoy the Victorian Parlour Songs and have been privileged to win the Katie Ayers Trophy in the past amongst others. I have been known to try and return the wrong trophy to the wrong festival! One trophy I am particularly proud of was the shield for the most entertaining performance in 2008 - Miss Hooligan's Christmas Cake!

I never won much at school, a history prize one year when I chose a book about Rommell and it was presented to me by Montgomery......

Competing in the Festival is a lovely experience, it gives a sense of achievement even when I don't win the class - people congratulate you and say they have enjoyed your performance, I would encourage anyone to enter and try their best. You need to be keen to take part and want to do it, get a good teacher, practice and work hard.

I am looking forward to 2011 and the celebrations of the centenary.

**Jonathan Morell, Competitor**

My earliest memory is of the piano - the huge, vibrant black and white keys, the polished wood reflecting my face in the sunlight. I started to play the piano when I was 5 years old, being taught by Barbara Fordham (my Grandma) who opened my deposit account in the huge bank of music. Then, two years later, at seven years of age, I was entered into the Southend Musical Festival and ever since then I have entered the Festival in a vast array of different classes, but all based around the piano. From the Jazz Class to the Own Choice (age group) classes I've always had the excited nervousness associated with performing and the adjudicators' comments have always encouraged me to come back for another bite of the cherry the next year round. I've had the joy of being brought up in a musical family, and thus have been able to enter the Family Class with my sister, Abby, accompanying her singing. I think this is definitely the most nerve-racking class I've ever competed in because it was the first accompaniment I'd ever played and I not only had to be good for myself, like I was used to, but Abby was relying on me. However it was possibly the best memory which I associate with the Festival because of Abby's smile as we went up to collect our gold medal and trophy.

I wish the Festival all the best for the future and hope that, one day, I might come back as an adjudicator myself and inspire people just like me.

***Michael Lafferty-Smith, Competitor.***

Competing in the Southend Music Festival has been a very valuable experience for me and I'm sure will continue to be in the future. The first time I ever entered a competition was when I was 11 in 2008. I was competing for the Walter Tee trophy in the 'Singing and Playing class' and I can't remember a time where I was more petrified. I performed 'Wade in the Water' by Eva Cassidy and came out with a merit. I couldn't have been more chuffed! Despite the initial nerves as I waited for my name to be called, it was fantastic to be able to perform and entertain people once I started playing.

After this first performance, I continued to compete in the festival and on occasions I came 1st either playing piano or singing. Inevitably, I had more success in 2010 where I won a gold medal for the 'Junior Jazz Piano solo' (15 years and under) and received honours for the 'Own Choice Piano solo'. It was unfortunate that I could not compete in the singing sections of the Festival in 2010 as my voice was breaking but I hope to compete vocally this year in the festival's centenary anniversary.

Since 2008 I have still failed to forget my nerves whilst waiting to perform and I doubt the butterflies will ever stop flapping inside my stomach, but I find that this gives an edge to everyone's performance in the festival and this is why I find the festival to be such a valuable experience to any young musician.

***Rosemary Pennington,***
***Cultural Development Officer, Southend Council.***

I took part in many Southend music festivals as a child, mainly on solo piano, but also in piano duet classes, and as accompanist to other performers. (Years ago the festival had dance classes, and I also took part in those). I can recall the terror at times, as we waited for the class, and then sat through other performers before taking to the stage myself. Sometimes we had to wait in another hall as the class started, and gradually one by one got closer to the stage - waiting back stage as the person in front performed, and then it was our turn! I always thought it was unfair that the people at the start of the class got to hear most of the other participants, as we were allowed to sit in the audience after we had played, but the ones at the end of the class were waiting in another room.

The Festivals were excellent experience, albeit frightening at times. My piano teacher often insisted that I entered the sight reading class, as it was such good experience to have to read accurately and to carry on regardless of any mistakes. On reflection now, this was a very valuable exercise, and although there were only a very few people in these classes, they were very useful. I entered classes with friends from school, who had persuaded me to accompany them, and this introduced me to the delights of Lieder at quite a young age, although we only tackled the more simple songs!

I did win some cups, and over the years, members of the Boys' and Girls' Choirs have told me that they have won cups with my name on, which is a lovely reminder to me. When my daughter has won cups in the music festivals I have always looked in great interest to see who has won these cups in the past, and often they are people who are now making a living in music, either teaching or performing.

***Alexandra Kidgell, Professional Singer.***

As a young musician, Southend Musical Festival was always a highlight of my year, rather like Christmas. I looked forward to it, relished every second of it, and felt its absence when it was over. I competed as a singer, pianist, flautist and actress, attaining varied levels of success across my disciplines, but always finding it an enjoyable and beneficial experience.

My earliest recollection of the Festival, aged about seven, is of a Speech & Drama class at Southend Civic Centre, but my most fond memories are from the years it took place at Highlands Methodist Church in Leigh. It was a wonderfully intimate venue, where competitors performed on the same level as adjudicator and audience, and I always felt that everyone in the room was on my side (with the possible exception of the other competitors!).

Now, as I forge a career as a professional singer, the experiences I had as a participant in the Southend Musical Festival have proved to be invaluable. The opportunity to stand up and perform in front of distinguished adjudicators and musically erudite audiences, and to receive constructive criticism, has enabled me to become a mature and confident professional musician. I hope that it will continue to thrive, so that many more young performers can benefit from the wonderful opportunity it affords.

***Roger Humphries, Musical Director, Southend Choirs.***

Lillian Blunt was my grandmother and a great supporter of the Southend Musical Festival, and entered as many classes as she could for a great many years. She just loved singing and performing to an audience, and together with her close friend and accompanist Katie Ayers, would sing anything and anywhere. She was very proud of the cups which she won, and showed them to us with pride. She was also very proud of the certificates and comments sheets, and took the adjudicators' comments very seriously. Lillian died in 2008, just one month short of her 99th birthday, and she continued to enter the festival right up until a couple of years before she died. The festival was a great joy to her, and she and Katie would spend many hours listening to other classes and other singers with great enthusiasm and support. (At the age of 80+ she was entertaining "the old folk" at Saturday clubs, never even thinking that she might be older than them!)

***Penny Kidgell, Piano Secretary, Southend Musical Festival.***

My involvement in the Southend Musical Festival began in the fifties and early sixties, when, as a child, I competed in the piano, dancing and singing sections. I loved the dancing and particularly enjoyed playing duets with my friend Elizabeth. It was a very happy time as lots of my friends also competed. I remember the adjudicators being very kind and friendly.

Later, in the seventies and eighties, I spent many hours enjoying being in the audience, watching my children perform in the singing, piano, woodwind and drama sections. I know they gained a lot of confidence from these appearances which stood them in good stead for later in life.

When I retired from my job I decided I would like to get involved in helping to run the Festival, so that other youngsters and adults could continue to enjoy the opportunity to perform. I serve on the committee and help to run the piano section as well as organising the advertising in the syllabus and the programme. It is a great team, and there is a lot to do but it is very rewarding and most enjoyable.

Sitting in on the classes (often next to the adjudicator) is fascinating, and informative. The adjudicators have a lovely way with the children and adults and always try to be constructive and encouraging. I really look forward to November each year!

***Jena Pang, Piano Convenor, Southend Musical Festival.***

In preparing this piece for the centenary book I had a look at old newspaper cuttings and found some rather dubious photos of myself as a child. One is of my first festival in the early 1980s - I think I was about 6; I think you might agree it's sweet.

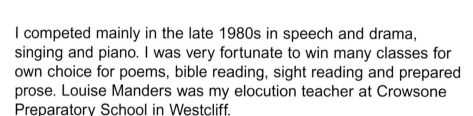

***Fig 83: Jena - very sweet!***

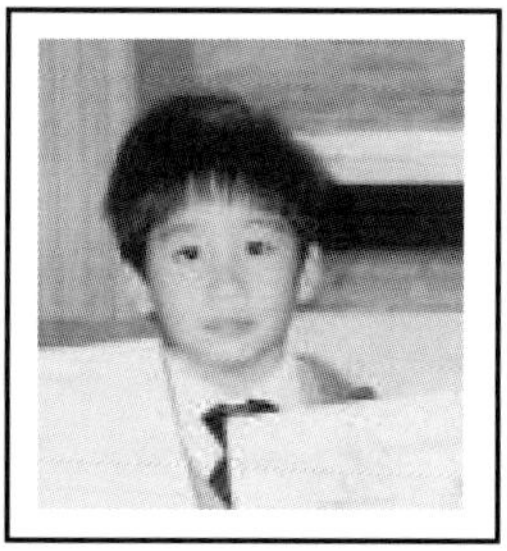

I competed mainly in the late 1980s in speech and drama, singing and piano. I was very fortunate to win many classes for own choice for poems, bible reading, sight reading and prepared prose. Louise Manders was my elocution teacher at Crowsone Preparatory School in Westcliff.

When I won the singing class, I sang The Wizard, I can't remember who it was by, but I attained 90 marks and the cup! I recall the class was held in a church and I was so excited.

I stopped competing so much once I started at Wesctliff High, and did not continue the speech and drama. I would have never thought that back then, I would be actively involved with the Festival and piano convenor!

**Elizabeth Elliott, Convenor, Singing Section.**

I have been associated with the SMF for as long as I can remember. My very earliest memory is standing on the high stage in Clifftown Church Hall singing under Mme Freda Parry in the Junior Co-op Choir at the tender age of 5 or 6! After that I started competing in the piano section - a very, very scary experience! Sitting in the waiting room out the back until it was my turn to go into the big hall up those steep stairs onto the high platform with the huge piano - I was terrified. I don't remember how well I did but I went back for more year after year after year...... I started entering singing classes in my teenage years with limited success and certainly could never in my wildest dreams have imagined that I would go on to become a professional singer and teacher.

One of my proudest moments at SMF was winning the prestigious FDL Penny Memorial Prize as a pianist in 1981 and then again a few years later as a singer. A rare and possibly unique achievement!

I moved away from Southend in the mid-80s, living and working in London and subsequently Florida where I had my two children Abigail and Jonathan Morell. On returning to the area in 1998 I immediately became involved with the Festival again as both a competitor and teacher, then later as a mother. I was extremely honoured in 2006 to be approached by Annette Forkin who asked me if I would consider taking over as Singing Convenor from Dorothy West who had sadly passed away at the end of the previous year. I have enjoyed every moment of my time in this role and am very much looking forward to our celebratory Centenary Festival this year.

**Sheila Kelleway, Vice Chairman, Woodwind & Brass Section Secretary.**

It was the musical career of my youngest child, Sarah, which led to my involvement with the Festival. In 1993 at the age of seven she began clarinet lessons with Gill Thorn and her appearances at the Festival started. She began with solos and duets and before long was a member of the West Leigh Woodwind Ensemble and then subsequently 'The Originals'. She also developed her singing career under the tutorship of

Clara Roberts. By the age of eleven she had become a seasoned performer and I was a very interested and keen supporter!

I volunteered to become a steward, a role which I still enjoy immensely. It is so rewarding to watch and follow the progress of young performers in all disciplines of the Festival. Over the years their confidence grows and they acquire skills that will stand them in good stead for the rest of their lives. In 2002 I was invited to become the woodwind & brass section secretary. I found this role a little daunting at first but soon understood how to book Adjudicators, liaise with the Convenor - Gill Thorn, deal with problems, assemble and move music stands and generally help to make the section run smoothly. Through this I have made new friends and have met many interesting people. I would like to thank Sally, Annette and Harry for all their help. The Festival enables performers of all ages develop their skills and gives pleasure to all. Long may it continue.

***Hilary Pell, Conductor, St. Bernard's Choir / Performer / Teacher***.

My first festival was in 1972 and a bit of a disaster!!! I forgot many words through nerves and felt I made a fool of myself. Somehow I was encouraged to carry on and continued to compete for many years. It was three years before I won a class. What made me carry on competing was the encouragement of my teacher, Margaret Cozens, and my parents. I did find the Church Hall, in, what was Clifftown Church, a rather unnerving place - the stage was so high and you could hear a pin drop in the uninviting hall. I know that the festival helped me to grow in confidence and work to a higher standard. I also learnt to control my nerves the more I did it. It was a good platform for me to experience and learn about myself as a performer and competitor. This, I'm sure, has held me in good stead when having to present myself in work situations and given me the tools to carry on developing my skills. I now enter many young people into the Festival myself as it helps their self esteem and gives them something to work towards. It's good to feel they can benefit from the experience as I did.

**Joanna Allnatt, Competitor, Professional Dancer Royal Ballet & Teacher**.

Though competing in the Southend Musical Festival was not my earliest experience of performing dance publicly, it provided me with an invaluable and timely forum for this. I had already competed in the Walthamstow Music Festival at the age of 4, performing one half of a tap duet whilst at the Alma Rippon Stage School. However, it was when I later joined the dancing school of Misses Dorothy and Constance Ellis of Thorpe Bay that my ballet training started in earnest, as well as learning the National and Character dance forms.

I was fortunate to be one of those selected by the Misses Ellis to enter the local festivals, following in the footsteps of quite a few of their previous pupils. As the Misses Ellis did not have a dancing school show during my time with them, the Festival gave us the opportunity to dance on a stage, get live audience reactions, to watch others perform and to receive valuable feedback from the visiting adjudicators. The encouragement and constructive criticism from these judges helped engender self confidence, but also a critical eye. Our own teachers' corrections to us were often repeated, reinforcing their validity in our minds. Going 'full-out' ("you only get one chance"), conquering one's nerves, carrying on at times of a momentary memory lapse:- also all valuable lessons for the young performer. Being selected from the semi-circle we stood in after the Competition class ended for a place and getting a medal or a mention was of course exciting and pleasing, and was and is an important external validation of potential and talent, but it was really the performing element itself and the surrounding 'buzz' which provided, me , anyway, with the most satisfaction. Also not to be forgotten was the first experience of 'backstage', with us getting into out costumes and having our hair and make-up done for us. I can still remember how the lipstick I used smelled !

At the age of 11, I went to continue my training at the Royal Ballet School and subsequently was invited to join the Royal Ballet Company, Covent Garden, with whom I danced for some years, both at Covent Garden and on numerous international tours. As well as the classics, I performed in ballets such as Balanchine's Agon, Ashton's Façade, and Tudor's Dark Elegies. I have since retired and have taught ballet to students of many levels, including at vocational schools such as Central School of Ballet, London.

I am very grateful, of course, for the support of my mother and others of my family and to the Misses Ellis for suggesting I enter the Festival and for the sound foundation their excellent training gave me. But my heartfelt thanks also go to all those organizers, supporters and volunteers, then and now, at the Southend Musical Festival, an event which has inspired and encouraged many young performers during the 100 years in which it has existed. Without this, who knows how many of us who went on to a professional career in the performing arts might otherwise not have done so? Long may it continue to flourish. Happy Centenary Year!

**Daphne Rowland nee Ventris. Concert Pianist, Teacher, Selection Committee.**

I started piano lessons at the age of six and was a pupil of Nellie Carrodus. I continued to work hard and practice a lot and eventually became a concert pianist. I made my London debut at Wigmore Hall in 1948. It was also in 1948 that I entered the Southend Musical Festival for the first time and I won the Chopin Cup. Ambrose Coviello was the Adjudicator and I still have his comments -'You set yourself an ambitious task'.

Life continued and I toured and performed with orchestras and was very lucky to have accompanied some wonderful singers and worked with excellent conductors.

When family life came along we settled in Southend and I became a teacher and my husband and I ran our own dance band - he was a percussionist. It was great fun. I also loved to sing and joined the Southend Choral Society where I met Madame Freda Parry and many other notable local musicians and singers, including Honor Jackson. Honor invited me to take part in the selection of pieces for the Musical Festival and I have been involved in that capacity ever since.

I enter my own pupils for the Festival and although it can be an ordeal the benefit of constructive advice from excellent Adjudicators is invaluable. I always try and give some helpful hints to my pupils for their performance - be smart, show off your platform manners, the audience is your friend, so go along and enjoy the experience - also always check the piano stool is in the right position!

The Festival provides a wonderful opportunity for young (and old) performers and I hope to continue to be involved as it enters its' next century.

**Denise Raynsford, Honorary Secretary, 1993 - 1997, Vice Chairman 1997 - 2000.**

I first became involved with the Festival in 1960. My daughter, Joanna, entered the dance classes and I met Pat Jacobson who also had a dancing daughter, Marcia. Pat was Convenor of the Dance Section and she invited me to help her. I eventually became Convenor myself. It was a lovely time, although the organisational side was really difficult. Everything was done by hand and the scheduling was a matter of spreading every piece of paper out on someone's floor and trying to sort them out into a sensible order! This was made worse by the sheer number of dancers in some of the group classes. It was a regular occurrence to have over twenty teenage girls in a group from some of the larger dance schools. I remember lots of clutter from the paperwork and lots of clatter from tap shoes, but we got there in the end.

Dance did appear to be the Cinderella of the Festival but it certainly thrived for some time, despite the uncertainty with venues and potential damage to wooden floors of 80 plus tap shoes. It would be lovely to see a new dance festival in Southend, even a one day event for small groups would be delightful.

As time went on I began to support Eileen Greaves in her role as Secretary and when she stepped down I stepped up. I think the best thing I ever did was to snare Annette in Waitrose and ask her to set up the computerisation of the Festival. The improvement in the workload and scheduling has been terrific. Another fabulous move forward has been the instigation of musicians and drama teachers in charge of the sections. I always felt a slight disadvantage as Secretary not being a musician myself. The Festival is a fabulous event, hard work for everyone involved but it gives great opportunities and satisfaction.

One of my favourite memories is when my daughter, Joanna, was five years old. She had entered a class and was performing to Little Red Riding Hood:

'What big eyes you have Grandma......'

(very expressive eyes)

'What a big nose you have Grandma.....'

(actions for elongated nose)

'What big teeth you have Grandma....'

(wide grin to bare the teeth)

At five years old little Joanna had no front teeth! It truly brought the house down.

My time as Secretary was a challenge, seeing the manhandling of pianos across icy pavements, feeding and watering Adjudicators, scheduling around a funeral at one point, but I would not have missed a minute of it.

**Pat Jacobson, Convenor, Dance Section.**

I became involved in the Festival through my daughter, Marcia, who entered both Dance and Speech & Drama classes. As an interested Mum I soon became involved in the organisation of the Dance Section and was Convenor for some time. As is usual with these things you meet other people and they get involved too. I became friends with Denise Raynsford and she helped me with the work.

We had such fun through our children and it has been so nice to be able to give something back. Twenty-seven years later I still help wherever I am needed every November. Whilst organising the Festival can be terribly fraught the fun far outweighs any problems.

One of the main problems that still exists is that of venues - in 1911 there was no suitable hall in Southend and in 2011 it still does not have an entirely suitable hall for the Festival!

I remember the manners & discipline at the Festival being impeccable, the children behaved beautifully. I used to stand in the wings and tell the children when to go on stage, the most awful thing was watching a child suddenly go blank and forget words or steps, I did feel for them!

My daughter was always entered into classes under the proviso that there would be no tears, she would do her best and if someone else's best was better on the day it was nothing to cry about!

One person who deserves a very special thankyou is Dora Patrick, she was the official accompanist for the Dance section and indeed for every dance school in the area. Her skill and dedication were absolutely indispensable!

It was a revelation to see just how much work is involved behind the scenes and as soon as it is over in November the whole thing starts again. I have met some lovely people and made some dear friends over the years and look forward to meeting even more.

**Barbara Fordham, Past competitor & Steward, Music teacher.**

I became associated with the Festival soon after moving to Southend in 1960 with my two young daughters. Having joined the Southend Choral Society almost immediately, I was introduced to the Festival soon afterwards. I began to compete in the singing classes - solo, duet, trio, quartet and I was also part of a very successful Madrigal class.

By 1969 I had four daughters and they all joined in with various amounts of success in singing, piano, flute and cello classes. Joy Elliott, my eldest daughter, entered both flute and piano classes but sadly passed away aged 17. My other three daughters have gone on to enjoy professional music careers and remember the Festival with affection despite the nerves!

Music is very prominent in the lives of a huge number of my family members and it is now a delight to see my grandson,

Jonathan Morrell, enjoying success at the Festival and my third daughter Elizabeth Elliott taking such an active part in the committee.

Many congratulations to the Festival organisation for its wonderful work, which I remember for half of the' centenary years, may it continue successfully long into the future.

**Lesley Williams: Director, Basildon Youth Theatre. (BYT)**

In the late 1980's I was working for the Prison Service and had hired a hall at the old Towngate Theatre for ex-prisoners to produce and perform a play. From that event the Basildon Youth Theatre was born. It operated an 'open door' policy and any youngster could join up. All the performers involved in the drama projects were disadvantaged in some way; they didn't fit easily into the society in which they lived. BYT gave these young people a focus, a security and sense of belonging, achievement and confidence. In the early 1990s our performing venue of The Bryn was burnt down and we were homeless. We continued to practice and work at my house, or the odd hall when we could find one, but essentially we had little chance of actually performing our work – then I discovered quite by chance the syllabus for Southend Musical Festival and there it was, our venue to perform!

At first we entered group classes such as the Choral Speaking and Dance/Drama and in the first year we did not do very well at all. Our main competition came from the Southend Focus Theatre group. The only success had was a dance drama called "The Agony & the Ecstasy" about the pain and joy of the Olympics. Listening carefully to the Adjudicator's advice BYT regrouped and entered again the following year. Entering every class applicable and won them all. The rivalry between Focus and ourselves developed into a healthy respect and even some collaboration.

The BYT reputation was achieved through the outstanding dance dramas in all age groups. Working hard to ensure that our dance drama pieces reflected contemporary themes of the day, Hostage taking, Disney Anniversary and for the Rugby World Cup the enactment of the 'World in Union' including the social problems of the World at the time.

Sadly, in 1991, two of my students became seriously ill and passed away. Hayley Cresswell is remembered with the Hayley Cresswell Cup for Dance Drama, which I will be presenting at the Centenary Festival. Jay Bagchi was commemorated by the group performing his story at the Edinburgh Festival.

Time went on and students got older and performance stopped for people to concentrate on GCSE and A level work. We then decided to turn professional and now BYT is an organization that visits schools, teaching and performing. BYT tackles contemporary and social issues, empowering young people. Many of the original performers are now parents themselves and a new generation of BYT is coming along. All the performers from the early days have continued to build careers in the arena of theatre – some professional actors, some teachers, one has started her own Youth Theatre in Manchester. Lifelong friendships and support networks were formed. Until we discovered the Festival the group was fairly isolated and insular, performing for friends and family, arranging fund raising events etc. The Festival opened up a new world that gave real validation. BYT never had a bad experience at the Festival, the students were accepted on a level playing field – a rare experience in itself for many of them. Competing brought a sense of teamwork and community to the young people who now work hard to give that same strength to the young people of today.

**Tina Davis – Speech & Drama**

I first became involved with The Southend Music Festival some fifteen years ago. My daughter entered as a competitor within the Speech and Drama section and as a parent I enjoyed watching the many classes that she entered over the years.

There is no doubt in my mind that with the encouragement of her drama teacher and through her participation in the Music Festival this definitely helped to give her the confidence as an adult that she has today.

So when I was asked to be Speech and Drama Secretary I was happy to offer my help. I am a relevant newcomer having only been active in the role for five years. I certainly could never have imagined as a parent the amount of time and effort that is put in behind the scenes by so many volunteers . I am very happy to be part of the Festival team and wish the Festival every success for its Centenary and for many years to come.

**Fig 84: Barbara Fordham & grandson Jonathan Morell. Starting young!**

**Sophie-Ann Chaplin, Competitor.**

My first Southend Musical Festival, in fact my first ever festival was in 2003 when I was eight years old. My first class was in the violin section and even though I had just started playing this instrument the adjudicator, Kay Tucker, awarded me a silver medal, I can still remember her telling me my performance was not boring. My parents were so naïve they entered me into the classes without an accompanist, so it was just me on my own and I loved it. That was it I had the bug for performing and I've never looked back. My next classes were in the piano section and I won a gold medal playing 'The perky parrot' by Alexander. I can remember a lady came up to me afterwards and said she loved my playing, it made me feel so happy that I could make someone smile with my music and I still feel the same today when I play. In the woodwind section I played my recorder and flute. The adjudicator was Jeffery Wilson, he was lovely and made me laugh. I didn't mind not winning I just remember being happy.

I was invited to play in the prize winner's concert and because it was my birthday on the same day everyone sang happy birthday to me and I was presented with a special prize by Mr Martin Gadd, who became my violin teacher. I have been attending the festival every year since then and have enjoyed every one. I have so many happy memories and have met many people who have always shown me respect as a musician even when I was very young. There is no doubt in my mind that the Southend festival has played and always will play an important part in my life as a musician.

# *APPENDICES*

***Southend Musical Festival***
***Executive Committee***
***&***
***Centenary Sub-Committee Members 2011.***

***Front Row: L to R: Sally Browne, Chairman; Annette Forkin, Honorary Secretary; Julie Lafferty, Author, Centenary Sub-committee; 2nd Row: L to R: Penny Kidgell, Piano Secretary; Ann Ridler, Centenary Sub-committee; Ann Jones & Sue Greengrass, Singing Secretary; Cherie Bason, Centenary Sub-committee; Kathryn Ash, Strings Secretary; Tina Davis, Speech & Drama Secretary; Back Row: L to R: Sheila Kelleway, Woodwind, Brass Secretary, Vice-Chairman; Louise Manders, Speech & Drama Convenor; Elizabeth Elliott, Singing Convenor; Harry Worsfold, Honorary Treasurer; Trevor Bason, Centenary Sub-committee.***

## Southend Musical Festival Officers:
## 1911 - 2011

| YEAR | Chairman | Vice-Chairman | Hon. Secretary | Treasurer |
|---|---|---|---|---|
| 1911 -1913 | HWL Hobbs | | Alfred Tarling | P.H. Kessel |
| 1914 | HWL Hobbs | J.R. Griffiths | Horace Bayliss | Chas Foster |
| **1914 -1919** | **No festival – WW1** | | | |
| 1920 | Alderman J R Francis | J R Griffiths | Horace Bayliss | Chas Foster |
| 1923 | J R Griffiths | James Sears | Horace Bayliss | Chas Foster |
| 1928 | | | R. Iliffe / L G Ling | |
| 1931 | James Sears | FDL Penny | Horace Bayliss | Chas Foster |
| 1936 | James Sears | FDL Penny | Horace Bayliss | Vacant |
| 1939 | James Sears | FDL Penny | Horace Bayliss | Vacant |
| **1939 - 1945** | **No festival – WW2** | | | |
| 1946 | Cllr. P B Renshaw | FDL Penny | Horace Bayliss | Herbert Bell |
| 1955 | Cllr. P B Renshaw | J.W Bates | Horace Bayliss | Herbert Bell |
| 1957 | Wilfrid A Waller | J.W Bates | Horace Bayliss | Herbert Bell |
| 1961 | Wilfrid A Waller | J.W Bates | Stella Sita-Lumsden | Herbert Bell |
| 1970 | Wilfrid A Waller | J.W Bates | Sheila Heppel | Herbert Bell |
| 1974 | Bernard Birn | J W Bates | Sheila Heppel | John Curtis |
| 1977 | Bernard Birn | J.W Bates | Rita Ellis | John Curtis |
| 1981 | Bernard Birn | J.W Bates | Eileen Greaves | John Curtis |
| 1985 | Bernard Birn | Peter Bayliss | Eileen Greaves | John Curtis |

| | | | | |
|---|---|---|---|---|
| 1986 | Peter Bayliss | Sally Browne | Eileen Greaves | John Curtis |
| 1990 | Peter Bayliss | Sally Browne | Eileen Greaves | Terry Peckham |
| 1993 | Peter Bayliss | Sally Browne | Denise Raynsford | Terry Peckham |
| 1995 | Peter Bayliss | Sally Browne | Denise Raynsford | Mark Perigns |
| 1997 | Peter Bayliss | Sally Browne | Denise Raynsford | Harry Worsfold |
| 2000 | Sally Browne | Denise Raynsford | Annette Forkin | Harry Worsfold |
| 2006 | Sally Browne | Denise Raynsford | Annette Forkin | Mark Bevenden |
| 2008 | Sally Browne | Sheila Kelleway | Annette Forkin | Harry Worsfold |
| 2011 | Sally Browne | Sheila Kelleway | Annette Forkin | Harry Worsfold |

# *SOUTHEND MUSICAL*

# *FESTIVAL*

# *TROPHY ARCHIVE*

Challenge Shield given by
the Musical Council.

***Fig 84: Challenge Shield.***

There is an archive book that contains details of all the cups, trophies and prizes given by the Festival. This appendix gives brief details of each.

## Choral Singing

**The Chas Waller Silver Challenge Shield i**
Chas Waller & Son, jewellers was the official agent to the Festival for the supply of cups and shields for over 40 years. This shield was presented at the first Festival in 1911. It was awarded to elementary school choirs.

**The Chas Waller Silver Challenge Shield ii**
In 1922 the choir class was split to give two classes, one for girls and one for boys. Chas Waller readily donated another shield.

**The Doreen Bowyer Prize for Children's Choirs & The Song Recital Prize.**
Doreen Bowyer taught music in Southend for 40 years. These prizes have been founded in her memory by her sisters.

**The Dorothy Ventris Trophy. (Contralto solo - 60 years & over)**
Dorothy Ventris had a lifelong interest in music and had a fine contralto voice. She was a member of Madam Freda Parry's choir.

**The Dulcian Madrigal Trophy.**
This award first appears in the programme in 1979. There is little known about its history. Hilda Nevard & Doris Jessett both conducted the Dulcian Singers.

**The Ellis Cup for Male Voice Choirs.**
This was presented to the Festival in 1975.

**The Freda Parry Presentation Bowl.**
This handsome rosebowl was awarded to The Freda Parry Ladies Choir at the Festival of Britain in 1951. The bowl was given to the Festival on her death and is awarded to the most

outstanding choir by the Adjudicator. The bowl has a permanent home at the Mayor's residence - Porters.

**The Girl Guides Association Challenge Shield.**
This shield was donated in 1936, our Silver Jubilee year.

**The H W L Hobbs Challenge Shield.**
This was the first trophy donated in 1911. Mr. Hobbs was the first Chairman of the Festival from 1911 -1914.

**The Hilda Nevard Challenge Cup.**
This cup was donated in 1960 by Miss Nevard. She was an active member of the Festival committee.

**The Hodges & Johnson Challenge Cup.**
This company was once Southend's leading music retailer. The cup was donated in 1955.

**The Lester Jones Challenge Cup.**
Mr. Jones was Secretary of the London Musical Festival. The cup was offered in 1933 for mixed choirs.

**The Mme. Radcliffe Lewis Challenge Cup.**
Donated in 1948 for Townswomen's Guild Choirs.

**The Mrs. Charles Waller Choral Trophy & Challenge Trophy.**
Mrs. Waller donated the choral trophy for Women's Institute choirs. The challenge trophy was donated in 1948 for small church choirs.

**The Mrs. E. E. Gayler Trophy.**
This trophy was first presented in 1957 for youth and club choirs.

**The Louise Boland Challenge Cup.**
This cup is presented for choirs of no more than 25 voices.

Louise Boland was an active member of the Festival committee.

**The Musical Council Shield.**

This shield is an original of the Festival. It was presented at the first Festival in 1911 for children's choirs.

**The Olive Owers Challenge Cup.**

Mrs. Owers was a member of the Festival committee for many years. This cup was donated in 1973 for children's choirs.

**The Pett Trophy.**

This trophy takes the form of four small cups. It is presented for vocal ensemble.

**The Phillip Leicester Parry Memorial Cup.**

This cup was presented for the highest marks achieved throughout the Festival and was presented by his daughter, Madam Freda Parry.

**The R.A. Jones Challenge Shield.**

Mr. Jones was the official Patron of the Festival from 1923. It is awarded to elementary school choirs from the infants' department.

**The Samuel Riley Memorial Cup.**

This cup was donated by the family of the late Mr. Riley who was a Festival supporter for many years.

**The Sheila Heppel Memorial Cup & Shield.**

The cup and shield were donated in 1982 in memory of Sheila Heppel by the Balmoral Singers. She was an active member of the Festival Committee for many years.

## Solo Singing Awards.

**Barbara Southwell Challenge Cup.**
Miss Southwell won the Gold Medal in 1937 and the cup was offered for the Senior Folk Song class.

**The Bernard Birn Challenge Cup.**
This cup was donated in 1961. Mr. Birn was Chairman of the Festival from 1974 - 1990.

**The Branchflower Family Challenge Cup.**
Presented in 1955. The Branchflower family were frequent and successful competitors.

**The Catherine Horder Memorial Cup.**
A highly successful competitor herself, this cup was donated by her family to be awarded to the overall winner of the Folk Singing classes.

**The Connie Wedderburn Cup.**
Donated by her daughters in 1984 and currently awarded to the Mezzo Soprano class of 19 years and over.

**The Doreen Bowyer Prize for Song Recital (£20).**
See above

**The Dorothy Havis Prize (£20).**
Miss Havis was Assistant Honorary Secretary from 1977 - 1993 and also official accompanist from 1978 - 1996. This annual cash prize was given for a class of duet for Voice and Piano, 18 years and under.

**The Dorothy West Challenge Cup & Memorial Prize.**
Dorothy West enjoyed a long association with the Festival as a competitor, committee member, convenor and accompanist.

**The Eileen Greaves Challenge Cup for Oratorio and Trophy for Family Class.**
Eileen was involved with the Festival for many years and donated two very handsome trophies.

**The Ellen C Petchey Memorial Cup.**
Presented in 1967 by Pamela Petchey, her daughter, for Songs from the Shows.

**The Emma Elizabeth Curtis Memorial Prize (£20) & The John Curtis Challenge Cup.**
John Curtis competed in the Festival for 60 years, he made his final appearance as a competitor in 1992 aged 78 years. The prize is donated in memory of his mother. The cup is donated for men's voices.

**The Florence Roaf Prize (£10).**
In 1989 a donation of £200 was given to provide a cash prize of £10 in the Junior Songs from the Shows class.

**The Frith Family Challenge Cup.**
Three generations of the Frith family have taken part in the Festival so far. This cup was presented in 1954 for girl or boy vocalists of 12 years and under.

**The G A Crow Memorial Cup.**
Presented in 1966 by Mrs. M. Baker in memory of her mother who had shown keen interest and support for the Festival over many years. Awarded for Junior Folk Song Class.

**The Gayler Challenge Cup.**
Phyllis Gayler was the Official Accompanist to the Festival for 50 years. This cup was donated in 1949.

**The Gilberts Challenge Cup.**
Gilbert's Pianos Ltd donated this cup in 1948 for the Senior

Lieder Class.

**The Gladys Butler Cup.**
This cup is awarded for Girl's solo singing ages 16 - 18years.

**The Grainne Ahern Cup.**
This cup is first mentioned in 1982 and is allocated for the Novice Class of 19 years and over.

**The Gwen Stevenson Challenge Trophy.**
Donated in 1958 and allocated to the Old English Songs class.

**The Horace Bayliss Memorial Cup.**
Horace was Secretary and adviser to the Festival for 58 years from 1914 - 1972. This cup was offered in recognition of his long standing - outstanding - service to the Festival. Awarded to a new class for any voice 18 years and above, own choice.

**The Mrs. H.W.L. Hobbs Challenge Cup for Ladies.**
Mrs. Hobbs was the widow of the first Chairman of the Festival. This cup was donated in 1934.

**The Ivy Wright Challenge Trophy.**
This trophy is a fine silver bowl presented for mezzo-soprano solo in memory of Ivy Wright, an outstanding mezzo soprano and Gold Medallist.

**The Jewish Choir Plaque.**
Donated by the Westcliff Jewish Choir in 1957 for International Folk Song.

**The John Hamilton Memorial Cup & Prize.**
John moved to Leigh in 1973 and became well known in the area as a singer.

**The Kathleen Willison Memorial Cup.**
This cup arises from another longstanding family association with the Festival. It was donated in 1957 and is awarded to the overall winner of the soprano, mezzo and contralto classes.

**The Katie Ayers Cup.**
This cup is awarded for solo singing classes. A local girl she excelled at music learning piano from Vera Harding. She was awarded three Chappell medals during the 1930s. Born in 1919 she was still competing at the festival with her friend Lillian Blunt in 1999 at the age of 90 years.

**The Leigh Operatic and Dramatic Society Trophy.**
Awarded for Songs from the Shows 1960 or later.

**The Lilian Wood Challenge Cup.**
Donated in 1949 for boys solo singing, 11 years and under.

**The Louise and Don Collard Cup and Prize.**
Lady Mayor of Southend on Sea 1986 - 87, her husband Don was a successful singer, together they supported many charitable and community projects.

**The M. L. Callard Memorial Cup.**
Donated in 1956 for Boys Solo under 11 years.

**The Mude Challenge Cup.**
Donated in 1964 for 13 - 15 year old singers. Mrs. Mude and her daughter, Gladys, were involved with the Festival for many years.

**The Peter Bayliss Memorial Salver and Award.**
**The Peter Bayliss Memorial Cup.**
Involved in the Festival since the 1930s Peter Bayliss, like his Uncle Horace, undertook any and every job to support the Festival and make it a success.

**The Premier Trophy.**
This trophy was first presented in 1987 for Solo Singing Premier Class. It is now awarded for the highest mark in the oratorio and opera classes.

**The Radford Cup.**
Solo singing 60 years and over. It is thought that this cup may have been donated as a memorial in relation to a local choir but no other details are known.

**The Sally Browne Cup.**
Associated with the Festival since 1978, and the current Chairman, this cup is presented for solo singing girls 16 - 18 years.

**The Sheila Heppel Shield.**
Sheila Heppel had a long association with the Festival. She was Secretary from 1969 - 1977. On her death in 1981 the Balmoral Singers donated the shield in her memory. It is awarded to the winner of the Ladies Vocal Trio.

**The Songs from the Shows Shield (Viccars Family).**
This shield is awared to the under 11 years class and was presented by the family of Jenny Viccars, a very successful young competitor in the singing section.

**The Tunnicliffe Trophy.**
Mrs. Tunnicliffe was Headmistress of St. Hilda's School. This trophy is awarded for under 9 years, girl's solo singing.

**The Vera Harding Memorial Prize (£10).**
A longstanding supporter and executive member of the Festival for many years this prize is given for an instrumental or vocal class each year.

## Woodwind (Recorders & Brass)

**The A F Ellis Cup (Woodwind Solo)**
Miss Ellis joined the selection committee for Woodwind in 1976. At this time she offered this cup.

**The Avril Dankworth Cup.**
Miss Dankworth presented this cup in 1983. It was to be awarded in the Treble Recorder Solo Class, 11 years and under.

**The Bill Lewington Musical Instruments Challenge Cup.**
This trophy was donated in 2000 by the renowned musical instruments company.

**The Chris Stevens Challenge Shield.**
The Chris Stevens Music Centre presented two cups in 1975. One for Brass Solo to be kept by the winner and one for Brass Ensemble to be held for one year.

**The Doreen Bowyer Prize for Recorder Recital. (£20)**
See above.

**The Eileen M. E. Neath Challenge Cup.**
The Neath family had been associated with the Festival for many years. Eileen Neath served as a Piano Selection Committee member from 1948.

**The Gibbs Family Trophy.**
The trophy was donated in 2006 and is awarded each year to the winners of the School Ensemble Class.

**The Junior Woodwind Challenge Cup.**
Mrs. Rita Ellis, Honorary General Secretary from 1977 - 1980, & Ann Frances Ellis donated this cup in 1992.

**The HSBC Bank Shield for Woodwind Solo.**
Originally donated by the Midland Bank in 1999. The name changed to HSBC in 2004.

**The Ivy Morton-Maskell Memorial Prize (£5).**
**The Morton-Maskell Cups:**
Three cups in total covering recorder groups, consort and solo.

**The Music for Pleasure Trophy.**
In 1984 this trophy was awarded in a new duet class for guitar and any other instrument. It is currently awarded to ensemble, any woodwind instruments.

**The Peter Bayliss Memorial Cup.**
This cup was donated in 2000 by Peter's daughter, Margaret.

**The Price Family Junior Novice Brass Shield.**
**The Price Family Junior Novice Wind Shield.**
Mandy Price has been an active competitor in the Festival for many years. She and her family are keen to encourage those who are just starting out with their instruments.

**The Southend Musical Festival Brass Trophy.**
This trophy was presented by Mrs. Anita Philpott in 2002. It is given in the spirit of praise and congratulations to those who give an exceptional performance in the Brass section.

**The Winifred Hunt Cup.**
Donated by Miss Hunt in 1974 for descant recorder solo, nine years and under.

**The Gerald Usher Challenge Bowl.**
This ornate bowl is presented for the first time in 2011 the Festival Centenary year. Gerald had been a long standing member of the Executive Committee and served as regional respresentative to the Federation. This bowl is awarded for the Woodwind Chamber Music class.

## Strings.

**Allegro Music Vouchers.**

Allegro Music has stores in both Southend and Chelmsford and have supported the Festival with the gift of music vouchers for several years.

**Annual cash prize.**

Cash prize awarded by the Festival.

**The Clarke Challenge Cup for Cello.**

Mayor Norman Clarke donated this cup in 1976.

**The Committee Shield.**

This shield was a new award in 1998 for school orchestras of 11 years and under.

**The Cowan Cup.**

This cup was donated by Mrs. Lale in 1983 in memory of her mother. The Lale family were keen supporters and competitors in the Festival for many years.

**Dorothy Ventris Trophy.**

There are several cups and trophies donated by Dorothy Ventris. This one is awarded for Senior Violin Solo.

**The Golden Jubilee Trophy.**

This cup was donated in 1961 by the Neath family to commemorate the Golden Jubilee Year of the Festival.

**The Helen Thatcher Challenge Cup.**

Originally awarded for Children's Percussion Band in 1935, this cup has been awarded to the best performance in violin aged 14 years and under since 1972.

**The HSBC Trophies for String Groups.**

HSBC sponsored two new classes in 2004.

**The Jena Pang - Brenda Farrow Rose Bowl.**
**The Jena Pang Prize for Junior Violin Solo.**
**The Jena Pang Prize for Senior Strings Recital.**

Jena is a current member of the Executive Committee of the Festival. He competed for several years before studying music at Oxford. Brenda Farrow was his violin teacher.

**The Jerry Mayes Challenge Cup.**

This cup was originally awarded from 1960 in Accordion classes. It is now awarded for Guitar.

**The Joyce & Bobby Birn Memorial Prize. (£25).**

Both Joyce & Bobby Birn were keen supporters not only of the Festival but also many other musical societies in Southend. Bobby was Chairman of the Festival from 1974 - 1989.

**The Leona Phillips Challenge Cup.**

Awarded to Junior Accordion from 1962. When the accordion classes ceased in 1972 this cup transferred to the Strings section.

**The Marjorie Bose Memorial Cup.**

This cup is awarded for best performance by a young violin / viola player aged 11 - 13 years.

**The Music for Pleasure Shield.**

This is the second shield of its kind. Donated for the Concert Band class.

**Mr. R.C. Howson Prize. (£10).**

This prize has been awarded since 1995.

**The Robert Carrodus Memorial Bowl.**
This bowl is awarded in the concerto class for violin and viola.

**The Sheila Marshall Memorial Cup.**
Arthur Marshall was convenor of the Woodwind and Brass Section for many years. This cup was donated in memory of his wife in 1995.

**The Southend on Sea Chamber Music Challenge Cup & Prizes.**
The Chamber Music Society has been supporting the Festival since 1950.

**The Wilfrid Waller Memorial Cup.**
Wilfrid Waller was Chairman of the Festival from 1956 - 1974. This cup was donated by Mrs. Waller in 1982. It is awarded in the Violin Solo class, 10 - 11 year olds.

**The Winifred French Challenge Cup.**
Miss French donated this cup in 1972 for duet for Piano and any orchestral instrument, any age.

**The Winifred Nancarrow Challenge Cup.**
Winifred Nancarrow had a long association with the Festival as a child competitor, a teacher and a member of the Executive Committee. This cup was first presented in 1950.

## Pianoforte.

**The Agnes Bateson Memorial Cup.**
This cup has been awarded since 1986 for the Chopin Junior Class.

**The Alfred Music Prizes.**
These four prizes were donated in 1998. Alfred Music have supported the Festival for many years.

**Allegro Music Vouchers.**

Allegro Music has stores in both Southend and Chelmsford and have supported the Festival with the gift of music vouchers for several years.

**The Amy Cheung Challenge Cup.**

Amy Cheung is a keen supporter of the Festival and of young musicians. Her son is Jena Pang.

**Annual Cash Prizes (£20).**

These prizes are awarded in recognition of competitors progression to the senior classes of Bach and Beethoven.

**The Benney Memorial Cup & Prize.**

This cup was donated in memory of Mrs. Benney.

**The Clare Christison Challenge Cup & Trophy.**

These have been presented since 1959 for Mozart lovers.

**The D. J. Rowland Challenge Cup.**

This cup, donated in 1975, is awarded for the highest mark in the Senior Piano Duet Class.

**The Dorothy Bose Memorial Cup.**

This cup is awarded for the highest marks in the Senior Piano Classes. It was first awarded in 1962.

**The Douglas Oates Memorial Cup.**

This cup was offered in memory of Douglas Oates who lost his life in the second world war and had been a regular competitor in the Festival.

**The Eileen Neath Prize.(£20)**

Eileen Neath was involved with the Festival for many years, from 1948. She was the organist at All Saints Church. This prize is awarded in the Jazz Class, 17 years and over.

**The Eleanor Button Challenge Cup.**
Presented in 1938 this cup is awarded in the Senior Beethoven Class.

**The Florence and Peggy Taffs Challenge Cup.**
**The H.C. Taffs Memorial Cup.**
The Taffs family have been associated with the Festival for many years. Miss Taffs provided the beautifully scripted certificates for cup winners. She was appointed an Honorary Member of the Festival in 2000. The memorial cup is presented to very young competitors.

**The Frank Bonner Cup.**
This cup is awarded for the highest marks across the Strings, Piano and Solo Singing sections.

**The Eve Garwood Trophy.**
Eve Garwood is a local piano teacher and Member of the Piano Committee & Executive Committee & Sponsorship Secretary for the Festival. This trophy is awarded in the Piano Grades 6 / 7 class.

**The H. J. Harding Memorial Cup.**
This cup was first presented in 1938.

**The Honor Jackson Trophy for Piano Playing.**
Honor Jackson was a highly respected local music teacher. She was Convenor of the Piano Section for 15 years.

**The Isobel Kennedy Trophy for Piano Nocturnes.**
Isobel Kennedy is a teacher of piano and strings and Member of the Piano Committe, Convenor of the Strings Section and Member of the Executive Committee of the Festival.

**The H.T. Neath Memorial Shield.**
This new trophy was received in 1967 for the Home Music Class.

**The Jena Pang Rose Bowl.**
**The Jena Pang Piano Concerto Award.**
**The Jena Pang Challenge Cup.**
See above.
**The Joan McCrimmon Cup.**
This cup has been awarded since 1982 for original composition.

**The John Stewart Memorial Shield.**
This shield was donated in 1984 by Mrs. Stewart in memory of her husband.

**The Katie Ayers Cup.**
See above.

**The Laura Matilda Bacon Cup.**
This cup has been awarded since 1977 for the Senior Recital Class (Open).

**The M. Lawton Challenge Cup.**
This cup was donated in 1947 for Chopin playing.

**The Le Hyde Memorial Cup.**
This cup was presented in 1962 by Mrs. Grace E. Upton to be awarded to pianists aged 7 years and under.

**The Margaret Helen Mills Challenge Cup.**
This cup was donated in 1995 for the Trio class.

**The Margaret Murray Challenge Cup.**
This cup was presented in 1960 for Junior Recital.

**The Margaret White Memorial Cup.**
This cup was donated in 1934 by Mrs. Leslie White in memory of her daughter who was a successful competitor at many of the Festivals.

**The Michael Lewis Silver Challenge Cup.**
This cup is awarded for the highest marks in the own choice Piano Solo ages 12 - 14.

**The Morton-Maskell Prize. (£9)**
This prize was initially listed as £3 in 1987. In 1995 it was agreed that the prize should be £3 for each member of the trio.

**The Muriel Muddiman Encouragement Trophy & Prize.**
Muriel Muddiman was a highly respected local music teacher and took particular interest in her very young pupils.

**The Mrs. Stevens Junior Challenge Cup.**
This cup has been awarded since 1937.

**The Music for Pleasure Shield: Clementi.**
Since 1984 this shield has been awarded for the highest mark in the two Clementi classes.

**The Norah B. Cable Challenge Cup.**
This cup is awarded to the winner of the Junior Bach Class.

**The Olive Redfarn Prize. (£10).**
This prize is given to the winner of the Beethoven Junior Class.

**The Mrs. P. Gollin Prize. (£5).**
Mrs. Gollin served as a steward at the Festival and offered this prize for Piano Solo, 8 years of age.

**The Phyllis Miller Memorial Cup.**
Phyllis Miller was a highly respected local music teacher and this cup is awarded to the Junior Mozart Class.

**The Piano Pavilion Trophy & Prize. (£50).**
The Piano Pavilion has been a supporter of the Festival since 2000. The trophy is awarded to the highest mark in the Piano Solo classes, 15 years and under and the prize goes to the winner of the Senior Recital Class.

**The R.L. Richardson Memorial Prize. (£25).**
Ron Richardson was a regular visitor to the Festival and a tireless behind the scenes helper, supporting his daughter - our current Secretary Annette - in her many roles. His bequest funds an annual prize in the piano section.

**The Rowan Jazz Trophy.**
This trophy has been donated by Margaret Rowan, who served as Convenor of the Piano Section from 2005 - 2010.

**The Vera Grand Challenge Cup.**
This cup has been awarded since 1950 for the best performance of one of Bach's preludes or fugues in the 16 years and over class.

**The Vera Harding Memorial Prize. (£10).**
For 70 years, first as a competitor and then as a teacher and accompanist, Vera Harding played an active part in the Festival.

## Speech & Drama.

**The Alice Jeffery Bible Reading Award.**
Alice was a regular competitor in the Festival, gaining confidence and honing her performance skills as a young child. She won the gold medal in 2003.

**The Anita Philpott Book Prize.**

This prize is awarded for Boys Verse Speaking.

**Annual Cash Prizes for Premier Classes.**

The Gold, Silver and Bronze Medal Premier class winners receive £20, £15 & £10 respectively. This monetary award is donated by the Festival Committee. The Gold Medal class has run since 1924, the Silver and Bronze Medal classes were introduced in 1947.

**The Cecily Moore Challenge Cup.**

Miss Moore was Convenor of the Elocution section and donated this cup in 1947.

**The Claire Angel Challenge Cup.**

Miss Angel was a member of the selection committee for elocution and donated this cup in 1933.

**The Clulow Challenge Cup.**

This cup was first presented in 1970 for verse speaking 17 years and over.

**The Daniel Radcliffe Cup.**

**The Gresham Cup.**

Marcia Gresham was a successful competitor in the Festival and donated both the Gresham Cup for Verse Speaking classes and the Daniel Radcliffe Cup - named after her son (AKA Harry Potter!).

**The Derek Lowe Memorial Cup.**

Derek Lowe was a playwright and poet. He was very involved in the arts and a founder member of the Southend Poetry Society. Following his early death at the age of 51 a new class was introduced for original poetry.

The Dickens Cup.

**The Dickens Fellowship Prize.(£20).**

This cup is presented for the best reading of Dickens in the senior class, the prize is awarded in the junior class.

**The Doris Freyer Cup.**

This cup was donated in 1956 for the Acted Poem or Story class.

**The Focus Ladies Rose Bowl.**

This cup is awarded to the winner of the Prepared Prose Reading class for 16 years and above.

**The Gold Medal.**

See above.

**The Hayley Ann Cresswell Challenge Cup.**

This cup was donated by the Basildon Youth Theatre in 1991.

**The Helen Thatcher Challenge Cup. (Dramatic Scene)**

This cup was donated by Miss Helen Thatcher in 1935.

**The Irene Creigh Challenge Cup.**

This cup is awarded for Junior Duologue.

**The Jackie Curtis Cup.**

Mrs. Curtis, a former Mayoress of Southend, donated this cup in 1988.

**The Julie Hall Memorial Cup.**

This cup is donated by Lisa Schneider for Verse Speaking 8 years in memory of her friend Julie Hall. It will be awarded for the first time in 2011.

The Kathleen Stone Cup.

This cup was awarded at the 1974 Festival for Verse Speaking, 14 - 15 years.

**The Le Page Challenge Shield.**

Miss Le Page was Headmistress of Alexandra College, a private boarding school located in Crowstone Road. She donated this cup in 1932.

**Les Voix Perdues Mime Challenge Cup.**

This cup was donated in 1983 for Solo Mime by Peter & Jill Monk.

**The Lottie Noel Memorial Cup.**

This cup was donated by Irene Creigh in 1959 in memory of her mother.

**The Margaret Stone Memorial Bowl.**

This trophy has been awarded since 1980 for a Shakespeare Class.

**The Olive Owers Plaque.**

Olive Owers was a member of the Festival and offered this trophy in 1974 for a Verse Speaking class.

**The Percy B Renshaw Shakespeare Cup.**

Alderman Renshaw was Chairman of the Festival from 1946 - 1956. This cup was donated in 1972 for a new Shakespeare class.

**The Prayer Book Society Prizes. (2 x £10)**

The Prayer Book Society introduced two age groups for the Cranmer Award, the overall winner would compete in the National Finals.

**The Ridley-Batchelor Cup.**

Peggy Batchelor gave this cup in 1960 for the highest mark in the Gold & Silver classes.

**The Silver Medal.**

See above.

**The W. Camm Bacon Memorial Cup.**
Miss Laura Bacon donated this cup in 1949 in memory of her uncle who was a keen supporter of the Festival.

**The W. V. Higby Memorial Cup.**
Mr. Higby was Headmaster of St. John's School, Billericay. The cup was donated in 1993 for Dramatic Scene, 13 years and under.

**The U3A Prize. (£10).**
This class was started in 1998 for Original Prose Competition, 60 years and over.

## The Centenary Cups & Prizes.

***Along with the usual extensive cups, trophies and prizes awarded throughout the Festival every year there have been several special awards donated this year to mark the centenary and beyond. Special keepsake glass trophies and money prizes will be awarded to the winners of our Centenary Classes, many of which specify set pieces which were included in the first Festival Syllabus in 1911. All of the cash prizes have been generously donated by Mr Peter Parsons.***

***The Festival keeps a trophy archive with much greater detail than I have been able to impart in this short appendix. The Festival is always delighted to receive awards for the classes and, as detailed in the chapters of this book, the cups and trophies are treasured and looked after for the benefit of all who compete. Each award is a part of the Festival's rich history and reflects the high esteem in which those who have donated such treasures were, and still are, held.***

## APPENDIX 3

### List of Figures.

**Chapter 1:**



**Chapter 2:**



**Chapter 3:**

**Chapter 4:**



**Chaper 5:**